A Guide to
the National Trust in
DEVON &
CORNWALL

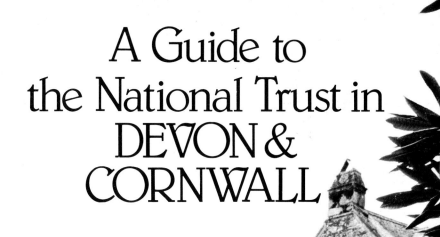

A Guide to
the National Trust in
DEVON &
CORNWALL

Peter Laws

David & Charles

Newton Abbot   London
North Pomfret (Vt)   Vancouver

TO MY WIFE
who helped so much

British Library Cataloguing in Publication Data

Laws, Peter
  Guide to the National Trust in Devon and Cornwall.
  1. National Trust   2. Historic buildings –
  England – Devon   3. Historic buildings –
  England – Cornwall   4. Devon – Description and
  travel – Guide-books   5. Cornwall –
  Description and travel – Guide books
  I. Title
  914.23'5'04857   DA670.D5

  ISBN   0-7153-7581-4

      Library of Congress Catalog Card Number 77–91765

© Peter Laws 1978

Set by Ronset Limited, Darwen, Lancs
and printed in Great Britain
by Biddles Limited, Guildford
for David & Charles (Publishers) Limited
Brunel House   Newton Abbot   Devon

Published in the United States of America
by David & Charles Inc
North Pomfret   Vermont 05053   USA

Published in Canada
by Douglas David & Charles Limited
1875 Welch Street   North Vancouver   BC

Contents

Publisher's Note

Not only is the South West one of Britain's most exciting regions but a unique proportion of its coast and famous houses and estates are owned by the National Trust. The range of Trust properties is indeed staggering. There is variety and drama enough even in the great houses wherein much of the West's turbulent history has been enacted. But the inventory includes a rich range of gardens outstanding in their own right, one-off jewels such as St Michael's Mount, some of the world's finest cliff scenery, a Dartmoor gorge – and much more.

Here is what might be described as a guide to the cream of an outstanding area, a book for tourist and resident alike. So rich is the cream that even those who have spent a lifetime frequently moving about in the two counties will discover much that is new, welcome the purposeful signpostings not merely to the places of special interest but what particularly not to miss while there.

Before founding David & Charles I was for many years holiday correspondent of the regional daily and always wished that a book such as this existed, for reference in the car and on the desk, for dreaming over in an easy chair and planning a fine day's expedition at the breakfast table. It gives me great pleasure to be associated with Mr Laws' work, brought to fruition with the encouragement and active help of the National Trust. Keep a copy in your car and lend it to anyone making serious acquaintance with Devon and Cornwall!

David St John Thomas

Introduction

The 1891 census of population in Cornwall was a little over 322,500, a drop of 47,000 since the 1861 census, much of it caused by the migration overseas of Cornish miners. The Cornish born architect, Silvanus Trevail FRIBA President of the Society of Architects, 1901–03, felt that something should be done to alleviate the economic distress at this time, and promoted a scheme to provide accommodation to attract tourists to Cornwall and turn the tide to one of prosperity. In 1891 he formed the Cornish Hotels Company becoming the secretary and architect and, in the spring of 1897, he designed two huge hotels that were to dominate the Cornish cliffs, the Headland near Pentowan Head at Newquay, and King Arthur's Castle on Firebeacon Down at Tintagel. This hotel was opened in 1899 (see illus 1) and a contemporary advertisement by the Company reads 'It stands on the spot where Tennyson received his inspiration for the Idylls of the King, a Palace by the Sea!'. Undoubtedly the erection of this very large hotel, still extant, was encouraged by the enterprising LSWR, whose North Cornwall line station had been opened at Camelford (for Tintagel) in August 1893. The hotel became so well-known that it was painted by Sir Edward Poynter, President of the Royal Academy 1896–1903, and hung at the Summer Exhibition in the latter year. Sir Edward, son of the architect Ambrose Poynter who had been a pupil of John

(*overleaf*) Location of National Trust properties in Devon and Cornwall

7

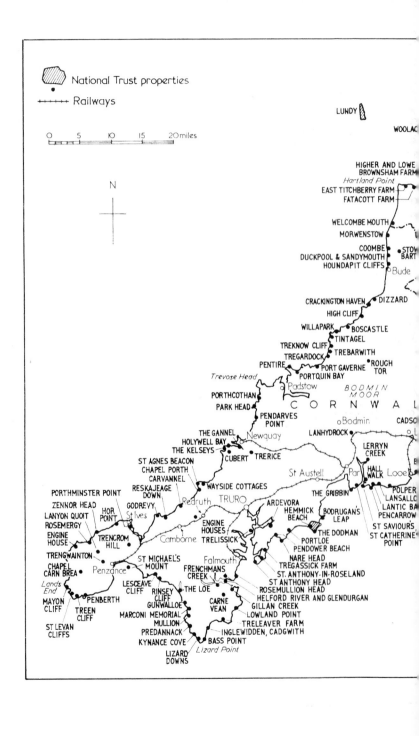

National Trust properties

Railways

0   5   10   15   20 miles

N

LUNDY

WOOLA

HIGHER AND LOWE
BROWNSHAM FARM
Hartland Point
EAST TITCHBERRY FARM
FATACOTT FARM

WELCOMBE MOUTH
MORWENSTOW
COOMBE   STO
DUCKPOOL & SANDYMOUTH   BART
HOUNDAPIT CLIFFS   Bude

CRACKINGTON HAVEN   DIZZARD
HIGH CLIFF
WILLAPARK   BOSCASTLE
TINTAGEL
TREKNOW CLIFF
TREGARDOCK   TREBARWITH
PENTIRE   ROUGH
PORT GAVERNE   TOR
PORTQUIN BAY
Trevose Head   Padstow   B O D M I N
MOOR
PORTHCOTHAN
PARK HEAD   C O R N W A L
PENDARVES
POINT   Bodmin   CADSC
THE GANNEL   Newquay   LANHYDROCK
HOLYWELL BAY
THE KELSEYS   LERRYN
ST AGNES BEACON   CREEK
CHAPEL PORTH   CUBERT   TRERICE
CARVANNEL
RESKAJEAGE   WAYSIDE COTTAGES   HALL
PORTHMINSTER POINT   DOWN   St Austell   WALK   Looe
ZENNOR HEAD   Redruth   TRURO   THE GRIBBIN   POLPER
LANYON QUOIT   HOR   GODREVY   ARDEVORA   LANSALLC
ROSEMERGY   POINT   St Ives   HEMMICK   BODRUGAN'S   LANTIC BA
ENGINE   ENGINE   BEACH   LEAP   PENCARROW
HOUSE   TRENCROM   HOUSES   THE DODMAN   ST SAVIOUR'S
HILL   Camborne   TRELISSICK   PORTLOE   ST CATHERINE
TRENGWAINTON   PENDOWER BEACH   POINT
CHAPEL   Falmouth   NARE HEAD
CARN BREA   Penzance   ST MICHAEL'S   TREGASSICK FARM
Land's   MOUNT   FRENCHMANS   ST. ANTHONY-IN-ROSELAND
End   LESCEAVE   CREEK   ST ANTHONY HEAD
MAYON   CLIFF   THE LOE   ROSEMULLION HEAD
CLIFF   PENBERTH   RINSEY   CARNE   HELFORD RIVER AND GLENDURGAN
TREEN   CLIFF   VEAN   GILLAN CREEK
CLIFF   GUNWALLOE   LOWLAND POINT
MARCONI MEMORIAL   TRELEAVER FARM
ST LEVAN   MULLION   INGLEWIDDEN, CADGWITH
CLIFFS   PREDANNACK
KYNANCE COVE   BASS POINT
LIZARD   *Lizard Point*
DOWNS

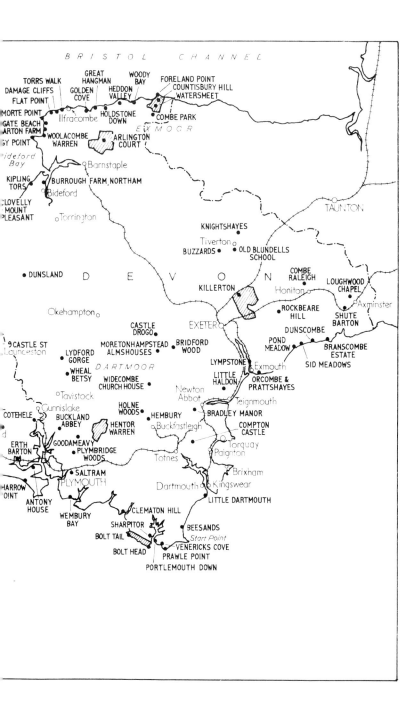

Nash and a founder member of the RIBA, had painted a series of murals at Wortley Hall Sheffield c 1880 for its owner the 1st Earl of Wharncliffe. The earl was a considerable landowner at Tintagel and his ancestor was MP for the area a century before. Lord Wharncliffe, it is believed, supported the hotel project. King Arthur's Castle Hotel was entirely a private venture, and was never owned by the LSWR, nor indeed by the GWR, for it was hostile territory to them.

The Headland Hotel at Newquay was not opened until 1902, its construction having been delayed by the Newquay Riots in August 1897. A crowd of local people, angered by the proposal to build a large hotel on unenclosed down on the cliff edge, had almost lynched the architect, an affray that ended with the leaders of the riot being brought to trial at Bodmin Quarter Sessions.

The building of these and other huge hotels on Cornish cliffs, (another was the Poldhu Hotel near Mullion) led to the launching of a local appeal in Tintagel in 1897 that resulted in the purchase by The National Trust of 14 acres at Barras Head, sometimes called Barras Nose, near the hotel site. This new body, The National Trust, was born in Grosvenor House, Park Lane, London (the then residence of the Duke of Devonshire) in July 1894, and registered under the Companies Act in January 1895 with the title 'The National Trust for Places of Historic Interest or Natural Beauty'. It acquired its first property, Dinas Oleu, $4\frac{1}{2}$ acres of cliff at Barmouth in Merioneth that same year, and its second acquisition was the 14 acres at Tintagel. '*A Minimis Incipe*' – From small beginnings!

Its founders were Octavia Hill, born in Wisbech in the Isle of Ely in 1838 to James Hill corn merchant and his wife Caroline, the Reverend Hardwicke Rawnsley, Canon of Carlisle and founder of the Lake District Defence Society, and Sir Robert Hunter, solicitor to the General Post Office and to the Commons Preservation Society, a body that delayed the building of the Headland Hotel in Newquay. Octavia Hill, by her mid-fifties, had years of dedication behind her in the cause of housing reform and saw clearly the dangers with which the spread of commercialism was threatening the countryside.

Illus 1 A Frith photograph of King Arthur's Castle Hotel at Tintagel which
was opened in 1899

The Trust's first acquisition in Devon was the gift in 1904 of 22 acres of heath and woodland at the top of Rockbeare Hill with the intriguing name of Prickly Pear Blossoms Park, lying 2½ miles west-south-west of Ottery St Mary (see page 119). Before some of the local authorities in Cornwall formed themselves into two Joint Planning Committees in 1936, when they adopted the Town and Country Planning Act 1932, there was absolutely no control over land use, and one has only to visit some of the 'developed resorts' of the 1920s and early '30s to realise it! As Michael Trinick, Secretary of the Devon and Cornwall Committee has written 'The GWR had been one of the pioneers of the holiday trade, and so promising were the auguries that the Company's Directors sought a new venture to increase traffic. They began to buy land between Saltash and Looe preparatory to opening up this largely under-developed part of Cornwall.' Indeed the Company proposed in 1935 to build an entirely new branch line from St Germans to Looe, but this plan was abandoned after World War II.

It was this threat that caused Treve Holman, then Secretary of Cornwall CPRE and Sir Arthur Quiller-Couch to start the preservation scheme at Lansallos that has continued to the present time.

During the past eighty years, the Trust have acquired throughout Devon and Cornwall over 40,000 acres of land, holding more than 150 miles of magnificent coastline, many historic buildings including twelve Great Houses, woodland and open spaces for public access on foot, prehistoric monuments, holiday cottages in Cornwall available to rent, and a number of splendid steam pumping and winding engines, products of the inventive genius of nineteenth century engineers.

This Guide will cover all the properties in the two counties, each of the chapters dealing with a particular type of property, but visitors will find it helpful to use in addition the Trust's detailed publications to some of the properties, which are listed on pp 13–14.

Devon

booklets
Arlington Court
Arlington Vehicle Collection
Bradley Manor
Buckland Abbey (not a Trust publication)
Castle Drogo
Compton Castle
Country Walks in Devon
Killerton Garden
Lundy Island (not a Trust publication)
Lydford Gorge
Saltram
Saltram: Catalogue of Contents

leaflets
Buzzards – a site on the Upper Dart
Coast walks in Devon
Killerton Estate – Woodland Walks
Knightshayes Court
Little Dartmouth
Loughwood Meeting House
National Trust in East Devon – properties in Exeter, Exmouth
    and Sidmouth district
Salcombe Coast Walks
Sharpitor
Shute Barton
Watersmeet
Weston Estate – coast walks Sidmouth to Beer
Woodland Walks in Devon
Woody Bay and Heddon's Mouth

Cornwall

booklets
Antony House
Cornish Engines
Cornish Holiday Cottages
Cotehele
Country Walks in Cornwall (published with Country Walks in
  Devon)
Glendurgan Garden
Lanhydrock House
Lawrence House Launceston (not a Trust publication)
Trelissick Garden
Trerice

leaflets
Cotehele: the 15th century Clock
Cotehele Mill
Tintagel – the Old Post Office
Trencrom Hill
Trengwainton Garden

In addition, the Trust have published a map, scale $\frac{1}{10}$in to 1 mile
of all properties, and an annual list of properties open giving
essential information for visitors is published. Westway Guides
publish *Motoring and Seeing National Trust Properties in Devon and
Cornwall* by Arthur L. Clamp covering eleven main properties. A
splendid illustrated history of St Michael's Mount, written and
published by the Hon John St Aubyn is also available.

1 North Devon Coastline

Watersmeet Estate

The most northerly tip of the county of Devon is Foreland Point
northeast of Lynmouth (see illus 2). Here the red gritstone cliffs
rise 900ft sheer out of the sea, and from a point a little over half-a-
mile southeast of the lighthouse built on the Point by Trinity
House in 1900 to the Sillery Sands southwest of the Foreland are
reputedly the highest cliffs in England. They are part of the Trust's
Watersmeet Estate of 1265 acres, acquired over the period 1934–71,
that runs southwards from the Foreland across the A39 Lynmouth–
Minehead coast road and down into the famous gorge of the East
Lyn River. A plaque in the gorge records 'The Watersmeet Valley
property acquired by the Lynton and Lynmouth Association for the
Preservation of Local Natural Beauties with National Trust
co-operation to whom it was handed over in September 1936'.
(See illus 3.)

Watersmeet takes its name from the confluence of the East Lyn
River with the Hoar Oak Water. The beauty of this enchanting
place was first 'discovered' by Shelley in 1812. Southey followed,
and soon it became one of the tourist meccas in Devon. At the
meeting of the two rivers, the Reverend W. S. Halliday of Glen-
thorne, (a romantically situated estate on the cliffs 3 miles east of

(*overleaf*) *Illus 2*   Foreland Point and Lynmouth Bay from Lynmouth

15

Foreland Point) built a charming cottage orné in 1832 to use as a fishing lodge. It is now Watersmeet House and is used as the Trust's shop, information centre and tea garden. The East Lyn is a notable salmon river, and there are seventeen special pools from Ash near Rockford Inn, Brendon, to Overflow, 2½ miles downstream.

Woody Bay

Woody or Wooda Bay lies 3 miles due west of Lynmouth, below Martinhoe where the Trust's 117 acres extend south from Wringapeak and comprise a mass of dense woodland that drops almost sheer to the sea 800ft below. Under an almost continuous tree-arch, a narrow lane, only practicable for those on foot (so leave the car at the top), drops down to the beach. The grandiose plan to cash in on the superb natural beauty of these cliffs (conceived at the turn of the nineteenth century) by developing them into a watering place, crumbled when its sponsor, a London lawyer, faced charges of embezzlement. It was he who built the pier below Martinhoe Manor (not a Trust property) to encourage the paddle steamers plying out of Ilfracombe, Penarth and Swansea. A limekiln at the back of the beach indicates an old landing place for schooners bringing limestone from Aberthaw on the South Wales coast for burning into agricultural lime.

From a hairpin bend just west of the roadside car park near Inkerman Bridge, the coastal footpath runs northwestwards along the landward boundary of the Trust's wood. About 630yd along this footpath there is a seat and from it, through a gap in the trees, there is a prospect of breathtaking magnificence that can scarcely be surpassed in all of the English coastline. Across Woody Bay, Crock Point, Duty Point, 4½ miles to Foreland Point, the cliffs rise straight out of the sea at a sharp angle, with large areas of woodland. There are splendid views across the Bristol Channel to the Welsh coast and the mountains inland. The coastal footpath continues westwards towards Highveer Point and on the summit there is the

Illus 3   The East Lyn River near Watersmeet, Lynmouth

site of a Roman Portlet or signal station established about the first century AD to watch for the approach of Welsh raiding parties from across the Channel. The path leads to Heddon's Mouth.

Heddon's Mouth

The beginning of another 941 acres of Trust land, acquired between 1963 and 1971, that includes 2 miles of coastline across Elwill Bay almost as far as the Mare and Colt rocks. The area runs southwards up Heddon's Mouth Cleave to Hunter's Inn, westwards along Trentishoe Combe to join up with the large open Trentishoe Down. Few coastal valleys in Great Britain have such a stark primeval feature as the great scree that forms the western slope of the cleft through which the Heddon river flows to the sea. From the summits there are exhilarating views, west to Widmouth Head, Ilfracombe, and across to the Welsh coast with, in clear visibility, a panorama from Worms Head, Gower, to Lavernock Point, Penarth.

Immediately west of the boundary on Trentishoe Down, the Trust has acquired 12 acres on Holdstone Down, a moorland rising to 1145ft above sea level. This downland is divided into numerous small ownerships and in order to secure a 'foothold', several plots were acquired between 1967 and 1970. In 1976, 56 acres of steep cliff were acquired on this down east of the Mare and Colt rocks.

The Great Hangman

Blackstone Point is 1½ miles west of the Trust's boundary at Trentishoe and is dominated by the Great Hangman, moorland rising to 1043ft. Here in 1972-3, the Trust was able to obtain nearly 300 acres of farmland, moorland and cliff with coastline extending to about a mile on either side of the Blackstone Point headland (see illus 4). The coastal footpath, inaccessible by car, runs through the property, and there are splendid views over the Bristol Channel and inland, southeastwards across Exmoor

Illus 4 The Great Hangman, Exmoor, and north Devon coastline east of Ilfracombe

National Park. All of these Trust properties between Foreland and Blackstone Points, over 2600 acres in all, are wholly within the National Park, doubly protected by Trust ownership on the one hand, and the strong conservation policies of the Exmoor National Park Committee on the other.

Combe Martin

West of the Great Hangman is the extraordinarily long village of Combe Martin that straggles for all of 2 miles along the valley floor through which the little River Umber flows to enter the sea at Sandy Bay. On the southwest side of this bay, at Golden Cove, an area vulnerable to 'development', one of Britain's foremost landscape architects, Dame Sylvia Crowe, gave 10½ acres of cliffland to the Trust in 1966.

Ilfracombe

The Handbook for Travellers in Devon and Cornwall (1865, Murray) describes Ilfracombe as 'a little watering place well known for the picturesque forms of the surrounding hills, its principal attraction the coast'. Nine years later, the railway arrived and the town rapidly developed into a big watering place! During World War II, the Trust acquired its first foothold here with 94 acres at Flat Point 2 miles to the west of the town. In recent years, a further 168 acres have been added along the coastline, comprising most of the Langleigh Valley southwest of the town, and the Torrs Walks, which were accessible in the 1860s 'by payment of a small toll'. There are views westwards to Brill Point, to the east of which lie the Trust's Damage Cliffs, an area of 113 acres of hillocky cliffs, once a golf course, acquired in 1968-9. There is access from the coastal footpath or on foot through Damage Barton farm.

The magnificent headland, Bull Point (see illus 5), where there is a brand new lighthouse, with 182 acres of land was acquired in 1973 and it unites the Trust's extensive Morte Point and Woolacombe properties with the Damage Cliffs to the east, thus making the Trust's ownership of the coast continuous for 5 miles. There is access from the lighthouse road and from Damage Cliffs.

Morte Bay

A Devonshire proverb says 'Morte is the place which Heaven made last and the Devil will take first', the point depending on the weather. In thick fog and Atlantic gales, its rocks have claimed a vast number of ships, yet in the bright sun the long expanse of Woolacombe Sand has an instant appeal. The Trust's first acquisition here was as long ago as 1909 and now its ownership extends to nearly 1300 acres, from Morte Point which is the northern horn of

Illus 5 Bull Point, north Devon, west of Ilfracombe

Morte Bay southwards to Baggy Point near Croyde. The beach, a huge sweep of sand, pale yellow in colour, is ideal for surfing. Behind on Woolacombe Down are wild flowers and butterflies, and Barracane Beach just north of the village of Woolacombe is famous for its shells. Whereas Morte Point is comprised of grey slate, Baggy Point only 3 miles to the southwest across the bay is quite different, being composed of hard sandstone and grits, and softer olive-coloured shale with fossils. There is a huge cave, Baggy Hole, under the Point, accessible at low tide by boat, and the views from the summit across the Bristol Channel to Lundy are very fine indeed.

Lundy Island

The Guide to this island says 'Isolated yet accessible, tranquil but not dull, remote but acceptably civilised'. It is an historic place, which was inhabited in prehistoric times. A Christian community survived here after the departure of the Romans in the fifth–sixth centuries AD, and four inscribed stones of this period are in the cemetery.

Its area is 1047 acres, 3 miles in length running north to south, an average of half a mile in width and almost entirely of granite, the final upthrust of a submarine mountain. The southeastern corner alone is overlain with Upper Devonian slate. The western cliffs, facing the winds that roar up the Channel out of the Atlantic, are 400ft high, and from here the land tilts towards the east where there are several small coombes filled with woodland, bracken, rhododendrons and hydrangeas.

Over the last century-and-a-half, three lighthouses have been built on the island. One in 1819 (now disused) designed by Daniel Asher Alexander, architect of Dartmoor Prison (1809), had its light elevated 567ft above sea level, the highest in the British Isles, and often obscured by low cloud or fog (see illus 6). It was replaced by the present North and South Lights completed in 1897.

In 1834, the island was purchased by a Bristolian, the Reverend William Hudson Heaven and inevitably became known as the

23

Kingdom of Heaven! He built Millcombe House, now a hotel, in 1836, and supported the opening of the granite quarries in 1863. They finally closed in 1911 and stone from them is said to have been used for the Thames Embankment. In 1895–6, his son, the Reverend Hudson Grosett Heaven, built the ornate Victorian church dedicated to St Helena, to the design of the well-known Victorian architect John Norton (see illus 7). It is an example of the thoroughness of the Victorians, its walls faced externally in Lundy granite, but internally in North Devon red bricks with a great deal of ornamental diaper work in blue and cream bricks and having a roof covered with Cotswold stone slates from Tetbury. All these materials were transported from Ilfracombe in the schooner *Kate* by the builders, Britton and Pickett of Ilfracombe.

In 1918 Lundy was purchased by Augustus Christie, father of John Christie of Glyndebourne; he sold it seven years later to Martin Harman whose children sold to the Trust in 1969, this being effected with the gift of £150,000 from Jack Hayward who lives in the Bahamas. It is now leased to and administered by The Landmark Trust who are preserving the unique character of the island. There are facilities for up to seventy persons to stay at any one time, in the hotel, the old lighthouse and five cottages, and access is by the Landmark Trust's vessel *Polar Bear* (200 tons), and also by the motor ship *Balmoral* between May and September from various ports in the Bristol Channel.

Westward Ho!

At the mouth of the River Torridge, on the west bank, the Trust was given in 1966–7 45 acres of farmland with access to two small coves at Northam. Two miles due west, to the west of Westward Ho! near Rose Nose the Rudyard Kipling Memorial Fund gave 18 acres of gorse covered hill, the scene of much of *Stalky & Co*. It is called Kipling Tors.

Illus 6   The lighthouse on Lundy Island designed by Daniel Asher Alexander and completed in 1819

Clovelly and Hartland

A century-and-a-quarter ago, Clovelly was described as the most romantic village in Devon, and probably in the whole kingdom. Its stone ridged street still draws enormous numbers of tourists in the season. The Trust was given its first acre here in 1921 as a War Memorial, and in recent years it has added another 588 acres of cliffs, woodland and farmland at the Brownshams, Fatacott Cliff northwest of Clovelly and Beckland Cliffs overlooking Beckland Bay. Higher Brownsham Farm is an ancient building with a late Tudor ornamented ceiling.

Four miles to the northwest, and a mile east of Hartland Point, the Trust acquired 120 acres in 1943 including a mile along the cliff above Shipload Bay. There is no access to the farmland of East Titchberry, but there is a car park at the entrance to the farm, where there is access to the cliffs at Eldern Point and down to the bay. See page 133 for details of a holiday cottage here. Five miles due south of Hartland Point the boundary between Devon and Cornwall runs down the valley that enters the sea at Marsland Mouth. To the northeast near Welcombe Mouth, the Trust owns one acre given in 1963.

Illus 7   St Helena's Church, Lundy, which was completed in 1896. Architect: John Norton

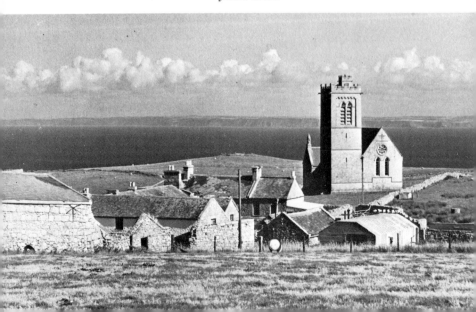

2 South Devon Coastline

Branscombe and Salcombe Regis

A mile west of Beer Head near Seaton is Branscombe Mouth. Here the Trust has secured almost 500 acres from Beer Head four miles westwards to Salcombe Mouth. Over the past twelve years this beautiful area has been acquired by a series of gifts and purchases with Enterprise Neptune funds. From Branscombe village itself a green valley leads down to the beach, but in the height of the tourist season the vehicles that use the lane are so numerous that considerable problems are caused by cars trying to get out while others are attempting to drive down, particularly when the private car park behind the beach is full. The situation calls for traffic management. Among the buildings to be seen are several rose-covered thatched cottages, two medieval farmhouses, one at Weston, the other at Edge Barton, the birthplace of Bishop Walter Bronescombe, builder of part of Exeter Cathedral between 1258 and 1280, the village smithy and, opposite it, a bakery that produces bread from an oven fired by faggots (see Chapter 10).

From the cliffs there can be seen, in clear visibility, the expanse of Lyme Bay, and a panorama southwestwards to Berry Head, Brixham, and eastwards to Portland Bill. Half way between Branscombe Mouth and Beer Head is a silhouette of Hooken Cliff, where during a night in March 1790, ten acres of land suddenly dropped

(*overleaf*) *Illus 8* Little Dartmouth, south Devon, and the mouth of the Dart

250ft vertically and moved 600ft out to sea, breaking up into columns and pinnacles of white chalk. From Branscombe beach, the huge rock at its summit looks like a fortress, and if viewed from the cliff top, this astonishing landslide will be seen at its most impressive. The cliffs along this stretch of coast are riddled with caves, many used by eighteenth century smugglers.

West of Salcombe Mouth is the attractive town of Sidmouth. Here the Trust has acquired 29 acres in three parcels. Peak Hill Field, Pond Meadow, and Sid Meadows which is part of a public walk along the river known as The Byes. Sid Meadows is the only parcel to which the public has access.

Exmouth

Between Exmouth Harbour and Straight Point 3 miles to the southeast, the Trust owns 126 acres comprising a mile stretch of high red sandstone cliff, known as the High Land of Orcombe, the foreshore east from the end of Exmouth Promenade to Sandy Bay, together with fields inland adjoining the ancient house called 'Prattshayes'. There is no public access to the house. Two miles north of Exmouth Harbour is the harbour at Lympstone. Adjoining the still-open railway station on the old Southern Railway branch line to Exmouth, are 6½ acres of Trust land overlooking the beautiful estuary with views across to Powderham Castle on the west bank.

Torcross: Slapton

At the southern end of the raised shingle beach separating Start Bay from the large Slapton Ley lies the little resort of Torcross. By the middle of the nineteenth century it was a place 'much frequented by the neighbouring gentry as a watering place', and the Dartmouth Coaching Company still owns the Torcross Hotel. South of the hotel the slate cliffs and rocks on the beach at Dun Point are contorted into weird shapes, and hidden in the cliffs is a fascinating old slate quarry, entered from the beach through a narrow cleft the width of a cart. This quarry was working in the 1860s when the local guide reported that the entrance was through a stone archway. With funds raised locally, this quarry and cliffland amounting to 16 acres was bought by the Trust in 1971.

Dartmouth

Apart from 9 acres of woodland at Dyers Hill including the old Ropewalk, the principal Trust ownership here is the magnificent area of 200 acres stretching from Gallant's Bower above Dartmouth Castle along $1\frac{1}{2}$ miles of cliffland between Sugary Cove, south of the Castle, to Warren Point. The cliff footpath affords magnificent views over Start Bay and the approach to Dartmouth Harbour. The car park is near Little Dartmouth Farm and from here the footpath runs down to the cliff. At Warren Point is a plaque commemorating the purchase of this land by the Devon Federation of Women's Institutes to mark its Golden Jubilee in 1970. (See illus 8.)

The Trust has made three spur paths connecting the bridle-way between the Coastguard Cottages and the car park, with the coast path, and on one of these spurs above Willow Cove, there is a stile that incorporates an ingenious lift-up 'paddle' to permit the passage of small dogs!

Salcombe

Between Prawle Point, the most southerly tip of Devon, and Bolt Tail, the Trust has secured since 1928 more than 1400 acres of cliffland on each side of the entrance to Salcombe Harbour. There is a continuous coast path on Trust land from Hope Cove to the Sharpitor Gardens, a distance of 6 miles, and on the east side of the harbour another 3 miles from Mill Bay to Gammon Head (see illus 9) and Maceley Cove; access is via the passenger ferry from Salcombe to East Portlemouth, or by car from the latter village. Finally there are the 13 acres at Prawle Point itself.

The walk along the cliffs from Sharpitor to Bolt Tail is one of the most beautiful coastal walks in South Devon. There is a par-

ticularly splendid view from the top of Bolberry Down southeastwards to Soar Mill Cove and the Ham Stone.

South of Salcombe town and above the South Sands is located
the Overbeck Museum in Sharpitor House to which is attached 6
acres of sub-tropical gardens. They were acquired in 1937 under
the will of Mr O. C. J. G. L. Overbeck who was descended from a
Dutch family, and who built Sharpitor in 1913. The gardens had
been started about ten years earlier and Mr Overbeck continued to

Illus 9   Gammon Head, south Devon

develop them on the terraces and by planting exotic trees and shrubs. The climate here is favourable to mimosa and agapanthus, and there are fine specimens of the Australian bottlebrush, *Magnolia cambellii*, the camphor tree from Japan, Chinese Tu-san palms, and the maidenhair tree.

Most of Sharpitor House is let as a youth hostel, but the remainder is a splendid museum. The hall has a South Hams cottage parlour of the nineteenth century: the Salcombe room illustrates the days when the Salcombe clipper schooners won fame for themselves, and the Overbeck room contains personal mementoes of the donor and his family. There is also an excellent natural history collection.

Just over $2\frac{1}{2}$ miles northwest of Bolt Tail at the beautiful mouth of the Devonshire Avon, the Trust own 7 acres at Clematon Hill, Bigbury-on-Sea, with views to Burgh Island and across the estuary to Bantham.

Wembury

Some of the special features of the coast of South Devon west of Prawle Point are the river estuaries, Kingsbridge, Avon, Erme, and Yealm. West of the village of Noss Mayo 6 miles southeast of Plymouth, at the mouth of the Yealm, the Trust were able to purchase in 1973–5, 442 acres of cliff, farmland and woods, making an almost continuous stretch of 2 miles of coastline from Mouthstone Point past Gara Point to Blackstone Point. The Countryside Commission made a substantial grant for this acquisition. In addition there are 27 acres of woodland to the west of Noss Mayo itself.

Opposite Mouthstone Point on the north side of the estuary, the Trust has acquired, since 1938, 86 acres between Wembury Beach and Warren Point, a stretch of $1\frac{1}{2}$ miles of coast. At the western end is an old water mill, now converted into a small refreshment house. Inside above the servery is an old oil painting depicting the building when it was used as a mill, driven by an overshot waterwheel, and part of the leat is still visible.

33

3 North Cornish Coastline

Morwenstow

The most northerly church and parish in Cornwall, originally dedicated to the Welsh Saint Morwenna, will for ever be linked with the name of the parson-poet who was Vicar there for forty-one years from 1834 until his death in 1875, Robert Stephen Hawker of Stoke Damerel. On the eve of his marriage in 1824, he wrote the Trelawny ballad 'The Song of the Western Men' in a cottage here and it became so popular that Francis Palgrave included it in his *Golden Treasury* in 1861. It is sung at hundreds of Cornish gatherings every year and has become almost an unofficial anthem.

On the very edge of the 450ft Vicarage Cliff is Hawker's Hut built of driftwood, where he watched the restless surge of the Atlantic which he expressed in his poetry. It was in the church which he served so long that he first introduced Harvest Festival.

Since 1959, the Trust has purchased here nearly 140 acres as a memorial to Hawker, farmland and cliff protecting the view from the church to the sea, a view that remains today much as it was a century ago. The 'Well' of St Morwenna on the cliff was built by Hawker; a St John's Well on the glebeland is very much older.

Bude

From Maer Cliff north of the town of Bude for 3 miles, the Trust now owns 1130 acres of cliffs and farmland. In the quiet and beautiful Coombe valley, acquired by The Landmark Trust, there are several charming cottages and a watermill also owned by this Trust. The whole is a happy example of cooperation between the two Trusts. An ugly bungalow on Duckpool Beach where the valley enters the sea was purchased by the National Trust and demolished in 1961-2.

Southwards from Coombe, the Trust purchased Houndapit Cliffs and Stowe Barton, a farmhouse on the site of the great house built by John Grenville Earl of Bath in 1680, a mansion that William Borlase the Cornish historian called 'the noblest in the West of England'. All that remains on the site are the stables.

A recent acquisition with Enterprise Neptune funds is the 115 acres on Maer Cliff immediately adjacent to the northern limits of Bude, and running north to Northcott Mouth to link up with the Trust's cliff acquisition between Menachurch Point and Steeple Point, Coombe.

St Gennys

Northeast of the ancient church of this parish is the Dizzard (anciently Disart) and here the Duchy of Cornwall gave the Trust 56 acres with a further half-share in 74 acres of Long Cliff from Dizzard headland to Chipman Point.

A mile southwestwards is the start of the Trust's 710 acres around Crackington Haven at Pencarrow Point, still known locally as Penkenna, from its Cornish name *Penkener* recorded in 1391. The Point shelters the little haven, where in the early nineteenth century small schooners were beached to be loaded up with local slate. This industrial activity promoted a scheme in 1836-7 to build a railway line from Launceston to a new port at Tremoutha, to be called Victoria, but it was abandoned. Here is the remarkable rocky point called Cambeak from the top of which there are magnificent views to Barras Nose at Tintagel. The largest block of land, 385 acres, was given in 1959 by Wing-Cmdr A. G. Parnall in memory of his brother and the aircrews who were killed in the Battle of Britain in 1940. The property includes the highest cliffland in Cornwall, High Cliff at 731ft. To the east was added in 1976 Trevigue Farm, 171 acres, and a sixteenth century house. There are magnificent coast views from the gated road that starts at Crackington Haven. There is a car park at the farm.

Boscastle

At Penally Hill starts the Trust's 500 acres at Boscastle Harbour and the Valency Valley, and its links with the novelist and one-time architect Thomas Hardy (1840-1928). In *A Pair of Blue Eyes* Hardy describes a dramatic episode set on High Cliff. In 1971 25 acres on the north side of the valley were purchased with money in part given by Miss Evelyn Hardy in memory of the novelist and his first wife Emma Gifford, whom Hardy met in 1870 when he surveyed St Juliot Church for restoration. She was the sister of the rector's wife.

Boscastle Harbour is like a miniature fjord, the only natural haven between Padstow and Hartland, and sailing vessels were often towed in by gigs. Penally and Willapark guard the narrow entrance channel to this most delightful of North Cornish harbours.

On Forrabury Common, the Trust own 67 acres, the common representing a unique survival of the Celtic tenure of land in 'stitch-meal'. It is divided into forty-two 'stitches' of which the Trust owns thirty-four. A 'stitch' is a long rectangular plot, cropped in summer and grazed in common in winter.

Tintagel

The Trust's first acquisition here in 1897, Barras Nose, has been mentioned in the Introduction, and during the past eighty years, the total acreage has been increased to 192. East of Barras Nose, the magnificent headland of Willapark with its cliff castle (not to be confused with another Willapark 2 miles northeast at Boscastle) was purchased in 1976. It embraces 1½ miles of coastline from Benoath Cove to Gullastem, immediately north of Bossiney. South of Tintagel there are 2 miles of cliffs running as far as Trebarwith

Strand and Port William. This was slate quarrying country and the quarry buildings on the cliff face at Dunderhole Point are now used as a youth hostel. Port William was a slate exporting haven like Crackington.

Just over a mile south of Trebarwith the Ordnance Survey map indicates 'The Mountain'. It is a menacing place around which a track curls to give access to Tregardock Beach under Tregonnick Tail. The Trust's 66 acres run southwards along the cliff almost to Jacket's Point.

Port Gaverne and Pentire

Port Gaverne is a charming cove lying immediately east of the much larger Port Isaac and was a haven for exporting slate from Delabole Quarry before the North Cornwall Railway arrived in 1893. On the north side of the cove in Trust hands is the old slate wharf and harbour wall. 16 acres here were given in 1958–9 in order to preserve the character of this delightful cove.

The cove called Port Quin, unsophisticated and unspoiled, lies 2 miles westwards and from here to Pentireglaze Haven the Trust owns nearly 700 acres. There are 40 acres of cliff and farmland at Port Quin, including cottages let for holidays (see Chapter 9), 106 acres at Lundy Bay surrounding Epphaven Cove, Carnweather and Pennywilgie Points, 364 acres at Pentire Farm including Pentire Point and Rumps Point, an Iron Age cliff castle, and 178 acres at Pentireglaze Farm.

The coastline from Port Quin to Rumps is unspoiled and beautiful. Stand on Pentire Point however and look southeast to Polzeath and New Polzeath. Here is the 'developers' paradise where, to quote Sir John Betjeman, 'caravans, railway carriage shacks and bungalows have done their worst'. It is one of the most horribly developed resorts in Cornwall, in fact it was so bad in 1936 that consciences were pricked to the extent that, when Pentire Farm was divided up into 'desirable building plots', a public appeal was organised by the Cornwall branch of CPRE and 362 acres were purchased for the Trust. It was the Trust's major acquisition in

Cornwall in the 1930s, and has saved a beautiful peninsula from nothing less than destruction.

1½ miles south of Pentire Point, on the Camel Estuary at Daymer Bay, 6 acres at Fishing Cove Field were acquired in 1964–7. Visitors to this area will find it rewarding, on a sunny afternoon, to have tea in the garden of Tregutt alongside the B3314 road 3 miles south of Port Quin.

Park Head

At Porthcothan Beach 2½ miles south of Trevose lighthouse (1847) the Trust purchased 17 acres on the north side of the inlet in 1967. A mile away is another Pentire Farm, off the B3276 coast road, where the Trust holds 222 acres including the fine headland Park Head and to its south Diggory's Island. The acquisition includes over a mile of coast, with eight small coves, a fine rock-arch, and a group of six round barrows. Southwards from the headland, there are fine views down the coast to Newquay, and close by are the Trust's 60 acres near the far-famed Bedruthan Steps, called Pendarves Point. They were given in 1930 by the late Charles Williams MP of Caerhayes Castle. The Steps are a stairway of stone cut into the cliff face, and were closed because the cliffs are so dangerous, but they were restored in 1975. The Trust has a new car park here.

Holywell Bay

The Gannel is a long sea inlet 2½ miles in length from Crantock Beach to Treninnick, lying south of the town of Newquay. In former times it was much used commercially. On the southern shore at Penpol the Trust's 640 acres begin, a splendid area along Crantock Beach, the bathing cove called Yugga, where access is from the path by the side of Crantock Church, round Pentire Point West (the East Point is on the opposite shore) to Porth Joke, Kelsey Head with its cliff castle, and so to Holywell Bay. Off Kelsey Head is an islet called the Chick which is also Trust-owned. 136

acres of this land are on Cubert Common, still fully grazed by commoners and the only enclosed common in Cornwall, or for that matter in England.

In the valley above Porth Joke is a variety of flora, and there are lime-loving plants on the cliffs, flourishing because the wind-blown 'sand' is composed of calcareous broken shells.

St Agnes

Dominating this old mining town, which was such an important part of Cornwall's mining past in the eighteenth-nineteenth centuries, is St Agnes Beacon rising to 628ft. From its summit, splendid views are afforded over 26 miles of the North Coast between St Ives and Trevose Light. Its 61 acres of heath were acquired by the Trust in 1956, and there are a few barrows. The Beacon has an extensive covering of prickly furze, so it is wise to keep to the paths, particularly if the family dog is around.

To the west and southwest is the Trust's holding of 363 acres, starting just south of St Agnes Head and running southwards nearly to Porthtowan, and including the narrow cleft of Chapel Coombe leading to the sea at Chapel Porth. This is an area ransacked for mineral wealth and the Trust owns some spectacular mine buildings (see Chapter 10).

At low water, a huge expanse of sand is uncovered and one can walk into a sea cave and look right up a mine shaft under Wheal Coates.

Portreath and Godrevy

The Trust acquired a splendid 4 miles of coast in 1939 between Godrevy Point and Crane Castle, and in 1961–2 acquired further land so that it now has a splendid foothold of 6 miles all the way to the Western Hill overlooking Portreath. All of this coast was part of the domains of the great Cornish family of Basset, who lived on the Tehidy estate nearby, one of whom was created the first (and last) Lord de Dunstanville in 1796. He died in 1835.

Along these 6 miles are delightful names, Ralph's Cupboard, Porthcadjack Cove, Reskajeage Downs, Hell's Mouth and Navax Point. Here is the haunt of the Atlantic seal and numerous seabirds, and Samphire Island where samphire is found. This was used by the Cornish for pickling, and can still be purchased at Wisbech from the Wash. The cliff top is 250ft almost vertically above the sea. At Godrevy Point can be discovered the royal fern and sea-spleenwort whilst half a mile off is lonely Godrevy Island where Trinity House first lit its lighthouse in 1859. It is an inhospitable place and the light has been automatic since 1934. The Trust's holding here is now 751 acres.

St Ives to Land's End

The only Trust property at St Ives is 12 acres at Porthminster Point purchased in 1961, consisting of cliffland parallel with the St Ives railway branch line between Porthminster Point and Carbis Bay.

The coast for a few miles west of Porthmeor at St Ives is composed of greenstone, before the granite is reached, and at Hor Point north of Hellesveor there was a threat in 1957 by the then local authority to use the point as a refuse tip, an almost unbelievable proposal. To avert this, a local family enabled the Trust to purchase 25 acres of 'a fine stretch of coast'.

The country now changes to the granite landscape of Penwith, landscape that the Hobhouse Committee on National Parks stated was fully up to National Park standards in 1947. Two miles west of Hor Point, the Trust's holding of 85 acres at Zennor is reached, 24 acres of cliffland north of Tregerthen overlooking Wicca Pool. Half a mile west again is splendid Zennor Head with Porthzennor Cove on the east flank and Pendour Cove on the west. 60 acres here were acquired in 1954 and 1968 and there is an excellent access road for pedestrians from Treveglos Farm in Zennor Churchtown. (The 'churchtown' is that part of a Cornish parish centred around the parish church.) In the church is the unique bench-end depicting the Mermaid of Zennor who, legend relates, lured the son of the squire to her watery home beneath the depths of Pendour Cove.

The entire granite coast of this part of Penwith is nothing short of magnificent, part of Britain's Heritage Coast, and indeed the 22 miles between here and Mousehole is claimed to be the longest stretch of granite coast south of the Cheviots.

Northeast of Morvah Churchtown the Trust was given a further 55 acres of this coastline at Rosemergy in 1958, in memory of the late Donald Thomas, first Chairman of the Trust's Cornwall Coast Advisory Committee. This matchless acquisition overlooks Porthmoina Cove to the northeast and the three Brandys rocks lie to the southwest. There are also four rocky viewpoints, known as Church Carn, High Carn, Osborne Carn and Towans Carn, all lying under the granite massif of Carn Galver. To the south of the Brandys is Whirl Pool.

Land's End is 'vulgarised with every device to part the visitor from his money', and the enormous weight of the tourists' feet is now wearing away the cliff top! Between Lands End and Pednmên-du a mile to the northeast, the Trust acquired 39 acres in 1935–6, including the Irish Lady Rock, and Maen Castle, the earliest known cliff castle, built c 300 BC. It has a single dry stone rampart. This land was given by benefactors calling themselves Ferguson's Gang, who composed a song for the occasion.

Up on the cliffs by Mayon Castle
What 'as you seen to make a fuss?
Up on the cliffs by Mayon Castle
There I seen the Octopus
What was the Octopus a-doing
East of the Longships as you go?
E'd some bricks and a load o'concrete
For to start on a bungalow.
Scarlet bricks and rubbery tiling
Bright red boxes all in a row
Tin ki-osk for the teas and petrol
Parkin' place for the cars to go.

Save me barrow, me old ring barrow
Take it safe to the National Trust!
Save me castle, me old cliff castle,
Save us all from the Octopus.

Ferguson's Gang will save yer castle
Save yer barrow and cliffs and you.
Thank you Sir, said the Irish Lady,
That is just what I hoped you'd do.

Tiddy fa lol, fa lol, Falady,
Tiddy fa lol, fa lol, fa lee,
'Ferguson's Gang', said the Irish Lady,
'Ferguson's Gang is the gang for me'.

(For permission to reproduce these verses the author is indebted to Ferguson's Gang.)

And so, a precious half mile of unblemished coast was saved, and the Treasury added a further 18 acres in 1964 accepted in lieu of estate duty.

4 South Cornish Coastline

Penberth

The finest cliff walk in West Cornwall is along the coastal footpath between Land's End and St Levan Churchtown, particularly the stretch along Ardensaweth Cliff. Above the beautiful cove of Porth Chapel is the headland Pedn-mên-an-mere (Cornish, 'the rocky head by the sea') which with 9 acres of the adjoining Rôspletha Cliff is in Trust ownership. The pressure to 'develop' this cove is still not abated, and this Trust foothold is extremely important indeed.

Half a mile due east of this headland is the well-known Logan Rock on its headland Treryn-Dinas. This huge rocky headland is a multi-period cliff castle, defended by a single curved rampart of great height with a bank and ditch across the final neck. The 'rock' is perched on top of one of the crags. Its 36 acres were given to the Trust in 1933 by Sir Courtenay Vyvyan of Trelowarren whose family had owned it since the twelfth century.

Since then the Trust's holding has been increased by a further 162 acres, 2 of them on the cliff above the beach called Pedn-vounder given by a French cable company in 1961. This company was originally called 'Le Compagnie du Télégraphe de Paris à New York', much too much of a mouthful for cable-key operators. It became the Pouyer Quertier Co, inevitably to cablemen the 'PQ' and the land they gave to the Trust was purchased by them as far back as 1874. Walk from the Trust's car park in Treen village

43

through the fields to Treen Cliff on a sunny morning, and then turn and look westwards towards Porthcurno over Pedn-vounder. The view is spectacular.

The Trust's remaining 160 acres extend from the cliff castle to Penberth Cove, a perfect Cornish fishing cove where their policy is to let the cottages they own to those who earn their living there, fishermen and flower growers.

Mounts Bay

The great sweep of this famous bay between Gwennap Head and Lizard Point is the setting for that place which is perhaps the most evocative of all Cornwall, St Michael's Mount, a Trust property since 1954 which will be fully described in Chapter 6.

To the east the Trust owns two small properties, 13 acres at the southeastern end of Praa Sands at Lesceave Por, and nearby 35 acres on Rinsey Cliff surrounding Porthcew Cove. (The restored engine house above the cove will be described in Chapter 10.)

Penrose

Hugh Rogers (born 1719) purchased in 1770 from a Mrs Cumming the estate of Penrose, near Helston. She was niece to and heiress of the last Penrose. In 1974 Commander J. P. Rogers made a princely gift to the Trust of the Loe Pool, Church Cove at Gunwalloe (2½ miles southeast) and 1504 acres. The Loe is a freshwater lake more than a mile in length, separated from the sea by a high shingle beach called Loe Bar, and generations of the family have established mixed plantations around the water's edge adding greatly to its beauty. The gift includes Penrose House but it is not open to the public, although the Penrose Walks beside the pool are open to pedestrians until dusk every day. Four car parks have been provided.

The coastline of the estate runs from near Porthleven for 2 miles to the southeast and the gift also includes Winnianton Farm which is of particular importance since its acquisition completes the ownership by the Trust of Church Cove, Gunwalloe (see illus 10), 128 acres being acquired here between 1956–9. The foreshore of 4 miles between Porthleven and Gunwalloe was also given to the Trust by Commander Rogers, together with a further 32 acres near Helston, in 1975 making up the biggest gift ever made to the Trust's ownership in Cornwall.

Illus 10   Gunwalloe on the Lizard coast, south Cornwall

Lizard Peninsula

The whole of this peninsula is a defined Area of Outstanding Natural Beauty, and between Angrouse Cliff, Poldhu and Lowland Point, St Keverne, the Trust has obtained 1070 acres since 1935. South of Poldhu Cove on Angrouse Cliff, Guglielmo Marconi leased a site in August 1900, built what then was described as 'an electric wave power station', and in April 1901 successfully transmitted wireless signals to Crookhaven in Co Cork 225 miles away. In Newfoundland, on that momentous day 12 December 1901, at 12.30 pm local time, he heard 'the faint but distinct successions of three dots in morse that had crossed the Atlantic from Poldhu', a distance of 2200 miles.

In 1937, the Marconi Company whose use for the site had ended three years before, cleared the site of its masts and buildings and gave 55 acres to the Trust. A Cornish granite monument stands on the cliff commemorating in four bronze panels the unique history of this place, where not only wireless was pioneered but also the Marconi-Franklin Short Wave Beam radio and the co-axial feeder cable, and where 'Puck's magic girdle round about the earth' was proved to be no idle boast.

Mullion Cove and Island with 11 acres was given to the Trust in 1945 and it includes the Harbour (built in 1893-5) that the Trust repaired at a cost of £5000 soon after they acquired it. The Winch House and a fishermen's store have since been added. North of the cove adjacent to Polurrian Cove, the Trust have acquired 5 acres of cliff including the viewpoint Carreg-lûz.

During World War II, the RAF established a large airfield on Higher and Lower Predannack Downs west of the A3083 road and south of Mullion. Here in 1968, the Trust purchased a great tract of 639 acres of typical Lizard scenery, heath, bog and rock, with rare plants and geological features. The coastal land runs from south of Predannack Head for ¾ mile overlooking Ogo-Dour Cove. North of this Head, the Trust also holds 5 acres of cliff with the headlands known as Laden Ceyn: Mên-te-Heul and Pedn Crifton. (See Chapter 11 for details of the nature reserve on 256 acres of this large area.)

80 acres of the Lizard Downs at and including Kynance Cove east side were given to the Trust in 1935 by the four owners, through the Commons, Footpaths, and Open Spaces Preservation Society. The coastal land extends southeastwards along the cliff overlooking the Lion Rock and Pentreath. Kynance has been famed for 200 years and although its character has remained intact, the hordes of feet that now come to it have caused considerable physical erosion. The Trust has just completed a new path up from the cove to overcome this problem!

East of Lizard Point is Bass Point, and here the Trust acquired $3\frac{1}{2}$ acres of cliff in 1967. Nearby, set in a Cornish hedge, is a bronze plaque depicting Marconi with an inscription recording his 'pioneer work for the safety of all seafarers', that was carried out in an adjacent building at the beginning of the century. Due north of Bass Point is Church Cove, Landewednack. From the lane leading to the Cove, there is access to 27 acres of cliff surrounding Parn Voose Cove, acquired in 1976.

Near the fishing cove of Cadgwith, the Trust purchased in 1966 a 55 acre farm, Inglewidden, with cliffs surrounding the 'Devil's Frying Pan'. Here the sea has eaten away a softer vein of serpentine to form a cave, the roof of which has fallen in, leaving an arch, behind which is a steep pit whose sides are almost 200ft deep.

In the 1820s, commercial working of serpentine started in this area, and following a visit to Penzance by Queen Victoria in 1846 when she admired serpentine and purchased a new table and other pieces for Osborne, a new factory was opened in the town, to be followed by the establishment of the Lizard Serpentine Co about 1853. Their factory, powered by waterwheel, was in Carleon Cove north of Cadgwith, and operated for about 40 years. The ruins of this factory and 45 acres of land at Poltesco and Treworder Cliffs were acquired by the Trust in 1974-5. From Carleon, the coast runs due east for several miles to Black Head, and to the west of the headland, at Beagles Point, the Trust purchased 112 acres of Treleaver Farm in 1966. Three miles to the northeast is the curious headland called Lowland Point, a relic of an Ice Age raised beach. The cliffs rise to 250ft half a mile inland. In 1956 a group of lovers of Cornwall gave the Trust 57 acres of farmland and wild cliffs, with views to the dreaded Manacles reef (in Cornish, *Maeneglos*, 'church rock') a mile to the northeast.

Helford River

Toll Point, Mawnan, on the north shore and Dennis Head on the south mark the entrance to the long wooded estuary called Helford River, which has its bridgehead 5 miles west at the port of Gweek, and a small wharf where several coasters berth every year with cargoes of coal. It is perhaps the most attractive of several such estuaries on the south coast of Cornwall. In all the Trust now owns 317 acres around its shores up to and including Rosemullion Head.

South of Dennis Head, Gillan Creek runs inland to Carne, parallel with the main estuary, and at Carne Vean the Trust has two traditional Cornish cottages of stone and cob. On the southern shore of Gillan Harbour near Flushing, the Trust acquired cliff-land at Trewarnevas in 1935, four years later the cove called Coneysburrow, and in 1965 a rocky promontory called the Herra, a total of $4\frac{1}{2}$ acres.

Southwest of Helford Point is Penarvon Cove, where the Trust owns 37 acres and three small cottages, the land being farm and woodland surrounding the cove, whilst a little over half a mile west is found Frenchman's Creek, its width diminishing until the tree branches meet over the water. This is the creek from which Daphne du Maurier's novel took its name, and the Trust owns 35 acres, 28 on the east bank and 7 on the shore of the main river.

On the north shore of Helford River, the Trust has acquired 184 acres since 1962 in the vicinity of Mawnan village. 100 acres are situated between Carwinion and Chenalls, southeast of Mawnan Smith, with pedestrian access down a long wooded valley to Porth Saxon, northwest of Toll Point, and another footpath from Chenalls eastwards, to the coast below Meudon Vean Hotel.

Southwest of Mawnan Smith is the estate of Glendurgan, its house c 1820, and 40 acres of wooded valley garden running down to the estuary (see illus 11) with beautiful trees, shrubs, water garden and a maze. They are described in Chapter 8 in greater detail. This beautiful place was given to the Trust in 1962 by members of the Fox family. In the tourist season, vehicles must park at Bosloe Farm where the Trust has made a car park. At the foot of the valley, the bequest also included eight cottages in the hamlet of Durgan.

Between Toll Point and Parson's Beach, underneath the medieval church of Mawnan, the Trust acquired 43 acres in 1963, cliffland with fine views from the headland of Mawnan Shear.

To the northeast is Rosemullion Head where the Trust has held 53 acres since 1939. The rocks are clothed with vegetation almost to the water's edge, and there is safe bathing in several coves, Gatamala to the northwest of the headland, and Prisk to the southwest.

St Anthony-in-Roseland

The parish at the eastern end of Helford is that of St Anthony-in-Meneage. The parish of St Anthony and its peninsula at the

Illus 11   Glendurgan garden, Helford River

mouth of the Fal is part of the Roseland district, and in this very beautiful and unspoiled area, the Trust has secured since 1957 a total of 690 acres.

The main block of 470 acres of coastal farmland and foreshore forms about half of the St Anthony Peninsula, including the hamlet of Bohortha, with three thatched cottages known as The Court (see Chapter 9). On the Channel coast, the cliffland includes the two headlands, Porthmellin and Killigerran, Elwynick Cove, and Porthbeor Beach, whilst on the Porthcuel River running north from St Mawes, a mile of the east bank and the southern shore of Froe Creek are also included. At the head of the Creek there is a dam, impounding several acres of water, formerly used to power a tide mill.

The southern tip of the peninsula is the headland called St Anthony and the Trust here acquired 35 acres in 1959–61, the site of the old St Anthony Coast Artillery Battery, established at the end of the nineteenth century as part of Falmouth's defences, and land adjoining St Anthony Lighthouse (1835) given by Trinity House.

On the eastern shore of the Carrick Roads, north of St Mawes, in the parish of St Just-in-Roseland, 45 acres were acquired in 1974–5 on Newton Cliff, running for half a mile along the cliff.

North of Froe Creek, the Trust purchased in 1968 the 143 acres of Tregassick Farm including the ferry point at Porthcuel, locally called Percuel, and has provided a picnic site at the viewpoint on the lane leading to the ferry from Gerrans.

Gerrans Bay

From the village of Veryan, a lane leads to Pendower Beach where a valley runs down to the coast. Here in 1961–2 the Trust purchased Gwendra Farm which comprises 247 acres overlooking the beach and the east side of the valley, and on which there are two famous ancient monuments, the great tumulus at Carne and an earthwork known as the Castle (see Chapter 11).

Nare Head

The eastern horn of Gerrans Bay is formed by Nare Head, one of the splendours of this part of the Cornish coast. The centre of the prospect northwest of the headland is protected by the Gwendra land mentioned above. The late John Charles Williams MP, who lived at Caerhayes Castle 4 miles to the northeast and was a benefactor of the National Trust, gave the headland and 109 acres in 1931. Since that year, the holding has been increased to 457 acres including the cliffland forming the southwest side of Veryan Bay, Blouth Point and Kilberick Cove. More than two miles of unspoiled coastline here, from Pennarvin Point northwest of Nare to Camels Cove near Manare Point southwest of Portloe village are now in Trust hands. The house Broom Parc (not open) in its little pine plantation is above Camels Cove. In this house the primate, Archbishop Cosmo Lang, spent much time in the 1930s. In Portloe itself, a still active fishing village, 7 acres adjacent to the Jacka were given to the Trust in 1944 to protect the amenity of the village.

The Dodman

Authors have written of 'the noble profile of Dodman' and it was the Dead Man's rock of Sir Arthur Quiller-Couch's novel. On its 373ft summit, there is a well-preserved Iron Age promontory fort, cut off by a very deep ditch called the Bulwark, and a tall granite cross erected in 1896 by the Rector of St Michael Caerhayes, to act as a mark for fishermen. Nearby is a tiny signal house for the coastguard with a lookout fashioned in the manner of a stone pulpit, possibly the only survivor of this early nineteenth century pattern.

In 1919 145 acres were presented by anonymous donors and a further 80 acres were purchased between 1964–6 to protect this splendid headland. The access is from a car park made by the Trust in the hamlet of Penare, three-quarters of a mile to the north.

The Trust's holding starts at Lambsowden Cove, where 70 acres

51

were purchased in 1969, and from here the coastline is in Trust hands for 3 miles round the headland to Penveor Point. Hemmick Beach east of Lambsowden was given or purchased 1957–66 with 53 acres, and there is access through a rock arch to Percumming Cove, the beach having waterworn pebbles of white, green, pink and brown.

To the north of Penveor Point on the east flank of Dodman, and not contiguous to it, the Trust holds a further 66 acres purchased in 1966 at Lamledra Farm Gorran above the curve of Bow or Vault Beach.

1½ miles northeast is Turbot Point, between Gorran Haven and Mevagissey, and here is the site called 'Bodrugan's Leap', to which there is access from the coastal footpath. A mile northwest is the hamlet of Bodrugan. C 1490 Sir Henry Trenowth of Bodrugan, a partisan of Richard III, was being hotly pursued by Sir Richard Edgcumbe of Cotehele, a staunch supporter of Henry VII; as they reached the Point, Sir Henry leapt off the cliff into a boat and escaped to France. For nearly five centuries the cliff has been called after this feat. In 1946 3 acres were given to the Trust by Mrs Guy Campbell in memory of her husband.

Fowey

The east flank of St Austell Bay is marked by the cliffs running due north and south from Polkerris fishing cove to Gribbin Head (see illus 12), its 244ft summit marked by the Trinity House day mark, a tapering stone tower 80ft high built in 1832, its three seaward sides painted in broad red and white stripes. To the east is the beautiful beach at Polridmouth Cove, south of the mansion of Menabilly, long the home of the Rashleigh family, and 'Manderley' in the novel *Rebecca* by Daphne du Maurier who lived at Menabilly for a long time. In 1966–7, 120 acres in this area, including the headland, were given to or were purchased by the Trust, thus preserving 5 miles of unspoilt coastline.

At the entrance to Fowey Harbour on the west shore is St Catherine's Castle built in the 1540s as part of Henry VIII's coastal defences that also included the castles of Pendennis and St Mawes. At St Catherine's Point the Trust holds 11 acres, 2½ at the summit and southern slopes behind the castle, given in 1919 as a memorial to Fowey men killed in World War I, the remainder at Covington Wood on the south side of Readymoney Cove given by the local authority in 1971.

To the north of Fowey overlooking the china-clay loading quays from Caffamill Pill upstream for half a mile, the Trust was given 31 acres of meadow and woodland, Station Wood and Carne Field in 1966.

Just over a mile to the north on the east bank of the River Fowey and opposite the village of Golant, 14 acres of steep bank were added to the Trust's estate by means of a local appeal in 1964.

From Caffamill Pill, a vehicular ferry plies across the harbour to the hamlet of Bodinnick, so long associated with the du Maurier family. Here starts the Trust's Hall Walk in Lanteglos (the Cornish name of the parish), 40 acres of land running down the east side of the harbour and along the north shore of Pont Pill. It was given in 1945 as a memorial to a great Cornishman 'Q', Sir Arthur Quiller-Couch of Fowey (d 1944), and to the men and women of Fowey and Lanteglos who fell in World War II. 'Q's' memorial is at Penleath Point on this land.

At the head of Pont Pill, the Trust has acquired 56 acres since 1955 on the south shore of the creek, and at its head. The footbridge and quays here were rebuilt in 1960 so that a circular walk could be effected from Bodinnick via Hall Walk to Polruan where there is a pedestrian ferry across to Fowey. At Polruan at the eastern entrance to Fowey Harbour, 4½ acres at St Saviour's Point were given to the Trust in 1926–33.

Lantic and Lantivet Bays

North of Bodinnick on the east bank of the Fowey is Mixtow Pill. Draw a line from here to Shag Rock 3½ miles east of Polruan on the

(overleaf) Illus 12 The coastline north of Gribbin Head looking towards Par

53

Channel coast, and there is enclosed a triangle of beautiful landscape and cliff scenery, the backcloth to Lantic and Lantivet Bays. Starting in 1936, 57 acres were purchased at Lansallos Cliff, and over forty years, the Trust's total stake in this beautiful place has been increased to 1129 acres. The coast from Blackbottle Rock eastwards for 3 miles to Shag Rock is all in hand, including the magnificent Pencarrow Head, its summit 447ft above the sea, with Great and Little Lantic Beaches below to the northwest and the several coves of Lantivet Bay to the northeast including Lansallos and Parson's. Inland the Trust ownership includes Churchtown Farm, Lanteglos, Triggabrowne and Frogmore Farms, Trevarder Farm northwest of Lansallos Church, and Lansallos Barton Farm to its east. The most recent (1975) acquisition includes Highertown Farm, standing high to the north and west of Lansallos, and completes the preservation scheme begun in 1936.

The Trust has provided car parks at Lansallos and Frogmore, and there is a lay-by on the south side of the road to Polruan above Lantic Bay. From this point a footpath leads to the top of Pencarrow Head where there are splendid views from Dodman to Rame Head at the entrance to Plymouth Sound.

Polperro and Looe

Of the cliffs east and west of the tiny 'fjord' that leads into Polperro harbour 1½ miles have been added over the past half century, which together with other land brings the Trust's holding here to 131 acres. On the western side of the harbour entrance on Chapel Cliff, because the cottages in Polperro are so tightly packed, some fifty plots (or quillets) were made on the cliff to act as allotments. Some are still let by the Trust for growing potatoes and flowers. At the Warren on the east side, 38 acres were donated under the will of the novelist Angela Brazil.

Two miles further east are the towns of East and West Looe and to the northeast of East Looe is Millendreath Beach at the end of a little valley. In 1967 30 acres of rough cliffs overlooking the beach with 13 acres of foreshore were given to the Trust by the

Metropolitan Railway Country Estates Ltd. This is the only Trust land here, and there is a good view southwards to St George's Island off Hannafore Point.

Whitsand Bay

On the coast southeast of Portwrinkle is a development that the National Trust guide calls 'the nasty chalet village of Freathy'! Immediately to its northwest are 284 acres of cliffs and farmland at Higher Tregantle overlooking Sharrow Point that the Trust was given in 1959–61. In these cliffs at the foot of the Point is a rock chamber or grotto called Sharrow Grot, or as the Victorians called it Lugger's Cave. It was excavated by a naval lieutenant called Lugger at the time of the American War of Independence, who gave himself the task of making the cave, 15ft deep by 7ft high with a seat cut in the rock, to cure his gout! The nineteenth century *Handbook for Travellers* says 'the cave is of no particular interest but it commands a delightful view'. It does not mention the fact that Lugger carved sixty-six lines of abominable and florid verses on the rock face, most of which survive! One mile to the west the Trust purchased in 1967 69 acres of Trehill cliff and farmland between highway B3247 (Antony–Crafthole) and the sea. A spur path connects the road to the coastal footpath from which there is access to a small cove. Nearby is the mid-Victorian Tregantle Artillery Fort, still used as a range and visitors are specially warned not to stray on to Ministry of Defence land when the red flags are flying.

There are over 300 miles of coastline in Cornwall between Marsland Mouth and Rame Head. About 103 of them are now in Trust ownership. One has only to look at New Polzeath and Freathy to realise what could happen, despite the planning authorities, if the best of this beautiful and much loved characteristic of Cornwall was in the hands of any organisation or individual other than the Trust.

5 The Great Houses of Devon

Arlington Court

Situated on the southeast side of trunk road A39 Barnstaple–Lynton, 7 miles northeast of Barnstaple, is the estate of Arlington with its mansion Arlington Court, set in the beautiful rolling countryside of North Devon. A few miles to the northeast is the Exmoor National Park boundary.

The Chichester family first obtained the manor here when John Chichester married Thomasine, daughter and heiress of Sir John Raleigh of Raleigh, North Devon, in 1384. The first of the family to live here was John who died in 1577. The foundations of his house can still be traced. When Miss Rosalie Caroline Chichester died in 1949 aged eighty-four she was the last of the family, and she bequeathed the whole estate of 3471 acres, her house and its collections to the Trust.

She was an unusual woman to say the least. Born in 1865, she became the sole heir of her father Sir Bruce Chichester on his death in 1881. In the 1870s she had been taken on long Mediterranean cruises in his yacht and she retained a love of ships for the remainder of her life. This fascination was extended to animals, shells and plants. She became a competent photographer, a prolific artist, and a great collector.

She made the park and much of her estate into an animal sanctuary and nature reserve. Her grandfather, Sir John, had planted the park and erected around it an iron fence eight miles long. She kept Shetland ponies, deer, donkeys and a flock of Jacob sheep whose descendants still flourish there. Buzzards and ravens nest in the woods and the lake is a wildfowl sanctuary.

The mansion was designed for Colonel John Chichester by a Barnstaple architect, Thomas Lee (b 1794), and was completed about 1822. (Lee also designed the Wellington Monument on the Blackdown Hills in Somerset in 1818.) Arlington Court is a severe neo-Greek building, relieved by a semi-circular Doric porch on the east front, and giant Tuscan pilasters at the corners. It was added to in 1865 by Sir Bruce Chichester, who cannot easily be forgiven for slighting so elegant a building. The handsome stables of the same date are far better architecturally than his extensions to the Court.

The interior of the house is distinguished for the suite of principal rooms on the south front linked by shallow arches – a feature of Soane's work in whose office Lee had worked for a short time – where the progression from room to room is marked by pairs of Ionic columns and imitation marble pilasters. The most delightful room is the Boudoir, facing west, an intimate little room with slightly coved ceiling and elaborate plaster decorations.

Undoubtedly, the main attraction of the whole house is the personality of the late Miss Chichester, expressed in furniture, pictures and her collections, all reflecting the tastes of her long tenure.

There are few works of art of the first importance, but a notable exception is a mystical watercolour 'Vision of the Cycle of the life of Man' painted by William Blake in 1821, and probably brought to the house in 1822. It was discovered by the Trust in 1949 lying on the top of a store cupboard in a disused wing!

To the east of the Court is the parish church of St James; its nave and chancel were rebuilt in 1844, and it contains a monument to Miss Chichester erected by the Trust in 1951, and designed by John Piper. It incorporates motifs of shells and ferns in reference to her interests.

The stable block to the east of the Church is an excellent mid-Victorian building arranged around three sides of a courtyard and housing an extremely fine collection of horsedrawn vehicles of every type. Visitors are able to enjoy rides through the park in several of these vehicles.

The close-mown grass paths are designed to take visitors to all parts of the estate, and will repay exploration. The walk along the front drive to the northwest of the house and thence down to the lake under Woolley Wood opens up lovely views over the coombe through which runs the River Yeo.

The entrance to the estate is via a lane leading off the A39 road. Here there is the car park, and a fascinating granary built in brick nogging and raised on staddle stones to keep out vermin. This building was taken from the Trust property at Dunsland near Holsworthy in 1967.

The popularity of Arlington Court is reflected in the number of visitors in 1976, 61,000.

Bradley Manor

Leading southwestwards out of the busy town of Newton Abbot is the main A381 road to Totnes. Half a mile from the town centre there is an early Victorian lodge on the northwest side of the road, and from it through a white gate without identification a winding drive leads to a stone wall with a gate and a bell. This is the simple and unpretentious entrance to Bradley Manor, one of the best examples of domestic Gothic fifteenth century houses in the West Country. The house stands in the sheltered valley of the River Lemon, and the estate of 68 acres is open free, and at all times, to those on foot. The house and garden, which were given to the Trust in 1938 by Mrs Alexander Woolner, are still the home of the donor and her family and are open at such times as are advertised by the Trust. All the contents of the house are privately owned.

The site of this historic house has been occupied since Neolithic times from the evidence of stone artifacts found near it. The very name suggests a pioneer Saxon settlement of the early eighth century, and before 1066, Bradley was part of the manor of what is known now as Teigngrace. The earliest part of the existing house is located in the centre of the south wing, and was built about 1250 by Robert Bushel. Here the family remained for five generations until the house passed on inheritance to the Yarde family of Malborough near Salcombe. It was Richard Yarde who built the main east wing with its great hall, solar, and buttery c 1420, and added the chapel in 1427 soon after the completion of the house. The building was in former times more extensive with an enclosed court to the east front and a gatehouse – an engraving of this is in Lysons' *Magna Britannia* (1814) – and further wings of the Tudor period to the west and north. All disappeared in the eighteenth century.

To the east of the great hall, the original porch was joined to the south wall of the chapel in the last decade of the fifteenth century c 1495, and it is this addition that has given bradley its picturesque oriel windows and gables on the east front (see illus 13).

Of special interest inside, are the medieval stencils and paintings on the walls of the 'banqueting room' (first floor: south wing), some of them black fleur-de-lys on a white ground; others the ihs monogram and Passion emblems. The chapel's barrel roof has sixteen carved bosses including a representation of Our Lord and the various arms of families connected with the house, as well as those of Bishop Lacey of Exeter who licensed it on 7 February 1428. Part of the original altar stone was discovered in the 1920s, and was restored in its original position in 1928, together with a delightful angel in alabaster that stood on the late Gothic reredos.

Next to the room where the wall paintings are seen, is the 'panelled room'; the panelling and plaster cornice, with cherubic and diabolic faces in the corner shells, and peas, acorns and other fruits in the swags, was constructed by Gilbert Yarde in 1695 for his new wife, Joan Blackaller of Sharpham.

The estate remained in the Yarde family until 1751 when it was sold, the historic old house subsequently becoming a farmhouse *and* two worker's cottages, the chapel a chicken run, and the great hall a barn.

(*overleaf*) *Illus 13*   The east front of Bradley Manor, Newton Abbot, c1495

In 1909, a descendant of the Yarde family, Cecil Firth of Ashburton, an archaeologist, purchased the remains of the house, and
then carefully restored them. In summer 1976, after being closed
for nearly four years, the house was re-opened, the repair work,
grant-aided by the Historic Buildings Council for England, included re-roofing with slate and treating all internal timbering
against decay and beetle attack. New wall paintings were also
discovered and they too were restored by a special Council grant.

One modern item inside the house is worthy of special mention.
As the visitor enters the buttery, on the wall facing the door is the
great steering wheel from the famous grain barque, the *Herzogin
Cecilie* that struck the rocks in Starehole Bay off Bolt Head in
1936, was beached and finally sank in January 1939 (see illus 14).

Buckland Abbey

The chronology of this historic site is as follows:

1278   Founded by Amicia (1220–c 1290) dowager Countess of
Devon and Lady of the Isle of Wight for the monks of the Cistercian
Order whose first Abbot, Robert, came from Quarr on that Island.
He was also Lord of the Hundred of Roborough and wielded
secular powers over an area that stretched from Lydford to Ply-
mouth and from the Tamar to Plym Steps.

The Cistercians were a breakaway from the Benedictines, and
were great farmers. In the fourteenth century their agricultural
estate at Buckland covering 20,000 acres was important enough in
the rural economy of West Devon for the Abbey to be fortified in
1336 against possible French attack.

1539   The Abbey was suppressed on 28 February and the Cistercian rule in West Devon ended. Abbot Toker received a pension
of £60 per annum, and his twelve monks smaller pensions or lump
sums, as little as £3.6.8 in some cases.

1541   The Crown sold the Abbey (ie the monastic church and its
immediate buildings and land) to Sir Richard Grenville, High
Marshal of Calais, for £233, and his son Roger became the first
secular resident. He died at sea in a naval action in 1545.

1576 Sir Roger Grenville's son was the famous Sir Richard Grenville of the *Revenge*, and he probably started to convert the still-extant monastic church into his house in 1574, keeping the nave and chancel retaining the great square tower, and inserting between the soaring walls of the church three floors to create living rooms, including a great hall. In that hall is a fireplace and over it Grenville inscribed the date 1576. The ancient church still remains, visible in innumerable details in vaults, arches and mouldings.

1581 Sir Richard retired to his old family home at Stowe in North Cornwall, and sold Buckland to Sir Francis Drake, on whose death it was inherited by his brother.

1643–6 First a Royalist stronghold still in Drake hands, and then captured by Fairfax in 1646, it was restored to Sir Francis Drake 2nd baronet at the Restoration, and remained with the Drake family until sold to Captain Arthur Rodd of Yelverton in 1946, through Captain R. O. Tapps-Gervis-Meyrick, a descendant of the Drakes, who had owned it since 1937. On 6 January 1938, a great deal of damage was done when the Abbey caught fire, but Drake's

Illus 14 The wreck of the barque *Herzogin Cecilie* at Starehole Bay, Salcombe, in 1937

Drum was saved and is still in the house, purchased for the nation in 1968.

1948 Captain Rodd gave the Abbey to the Trust so that it might be preserved, and it was then agreed that the Trust and the Pilgrim Trust, brought in by Lord Astor, should recondition the building, and that on completion, Plymouth Corporation should assume responsibility for it, and open it to the public as a Drake, Naval and West Country Folk Museum.

1951 After a great deal of work, the Abbey was opened as part of the Festival of Britain celebrations in July 1951, by Admiral the Earl Mountbatten of Burma.

Today it is a splendid museum and the old building, after seven centuries, has become a 'show-place, welcoming everyone as visitors'. One fascinating item is a replica of a brass plate, the original of which was discovered in California in 1936. This was set up at Point Reyes, northwest of San Francisco, by Sir Francis Drake during his circumnavigation of the world, between December 1577 and September 1580. It proclaimed in lettering punched into the metal that he had taken possession of the land as *Nova Albion* in the name of Queen Elizabeth on 15 June 1579. (Its authenticity was queried in a report from San Francisco dated 28 July 1977.)

On the eighteenth century staircase, with its gate at the foot to keep dogs out of the bedrooms, is the oldest engraving of the Abbey dated 1734. It could with advantage be positioned in a more prominent place.

On the east side of the main building is the very fine monastic tithe barn, for storage of tithes received from tenants and payable in kind. It was built about 650 years ago, and is 154ft long, 28ft wide and 40ft to the apex of the open timber roof. It is in excellent condition, and now houses a number of historic vehicles. These include a four-wheeled farm waggon from Berkshire c 1775; the Tavistock eight-seater horsedrawn station bus 1860–1910 and a post chaise c 1790, its body suspended by leather harness on 'C' springs. A post chaise was driven by postillions who rode the left hand horse, thus establishing our custom of driving on the left.

There is a fine garden of 3 acres around the Abbey and tithe barn, which are to be found 1 mile south of Buckland Monachorum, west of A386, the main road from Plymouth to Tavistock.

Castle Drogo

Leave the A30 at Whiddon Down (between Exeter and Okehampton) and drive towards Moretonhampstead on the A382. After about $2\frac{3}{4}$ miles, turn left at the hamlet of Sandypark in the Teign Valley. After about a mile, suddenly and dramatically, the majestic pile of Drogo is seen on a bluff 900ft up overlooking the Teign gorge, looking in silhouette not unlike Kenilworth Castle. After another mile, the high hedges bordering the narrow road suddenly open out into a circular clearing with clumps of ilexes. The drive to the Castle leads off to the right through a pair of clipped yews, treated architecturally like 'double lodges', and brings the visitor to the car park. The walk from here to the house gives splendid views over the gorge and Dartmoor National Park, and then, and only then, is seen the magnificence of this twentieth century country house, probably the last great private house of its kind likely to be built in this country (see illus 15). The preservation of country houses has long been one of the Trust's major preoccupations. To qualify a house must be of real architectural quality and if possible, the family, where there is one, should be enabled to live in it.

Drogo is without any doubt one of the most remarkable works of that great English architect Sir Edwin Lutyens (1869-1944), a building of the first quality, designed and built in this century. Located on the bluff above the wooded gorge, it is made entirely of Devon granite quarried near the site, and from its windows there are panoramic views over northeast Dartmoor and the farms of Chagford Vale. The donor gave 600 acres with the Castle and placed another 150 acres under protective covenant with the Trust.

The client for whom Lutyens worked was Julius Drewe (1856-1930) son of the Reverend G. S. Drewe, sometime Rector of Avington near Winchester, a fine church of 1779 that still retains all its original Georgian furnishings. Did this fine church have some

Illus 15   Castle Drogo, Sir Edwin Lutyens' great house built
between 1911 and 1930

influence on Drewe's choice of Lutyens?

Julius founded The Home and Colonial Stores in 1878 and by
1889 he and his partner, John Musker, had developed the business to
such an extent that both retired from active participation, Drewe
being only 33. In 1890 he purchased Culverden Castle at Tunbridge
Wells and then nine years later Wadhurst Hall in Sussex. In 1901
he paid several visits to Drewsteignton where his uncle Richard
Peck was rector, and it was then that he conceived the idea of
Castle Drogo, from Drogo de Teigne a Norman who gave his
name to the parish, and from whom Julius' brother William claimed
descent.

In 1910 Drewe asked Lutyens to accept a commission to build
his Castle; the price was to be in the region of £50,000 plus £10,000
for the garden, and the foundation stone was laid on 4 April 1911,
the client's fifty-fifth birthday.

The architect's enthusiasm for this massive project over-reached
itself to such an extent that Drewe and his wife realised by the
end of 1911 that the principal rooms as then designed were too
large to be comfortable. A drastic revision was necessary and this
was adopted by October 1912. Work then continued steadily, the
granite was quarried at Whiddon Park, transported to the site by
traction engine or steam wagon, and all the masonry was laid by
two masons, Doodney and Cleave, who finally finished their work

in 1930. The family moved into the nearly-complete house in 1927.

The house, both externally and internally, is faced with the finest silver-grey Devon granite, and above the front door is the splendid heraldic 'Mr Drewe's Lion', meticulously designed by Lutyens, and underneath in Roman lettering *Drogo nomen et virtus arma dedit*, the Drewe motto.

The rooms that are open to the public are the great hall, with its massive granite arches; the L-shaped library (the everyday sitting room); the drawing room, panelled and coloured in a soft green as a deliberate foil to the bare stonework elsewhere; the dining room with Harcourt's portrait of Julius Drewe; the kitchen and other service rooms — note the large Cornish range from the Redruth foundry of Terrill and Rogers. On the upper floor are Mr Drewe's dressing room; Mrs Drewe's bedroom; the boudoir and Adrian Drewe's room, with its souvenirs of Eton and Cambridge, a memorial to a beloved son killed in Flanders in 1917. The simple wooden cross that formerly stood on his Flanders grave is in the chapel.

This is a wonderful house, where to quote Michael Trinick 'dramatic architecture married to splendid scenery have been preserved together to unite the very warp and weave of the National Trust's tapestry'. A period of inspection in the house can be rounded off by a spectacular walk taking $1\frac{1}{2}$ hours, from Drews-teignton to Fingle Bridge, and thence by Hunter's Path dropping down to the Teign and back via Dogmarsh Bridge. During the first season (1975) this property was open to the public, there were 62,000 visitors.

Compton Castle

Almost central in the triangle formed by Newton Abbot, Paignton and Totnes is this fortified house of the fourteenth–sixteenth centuries, situated on the southwest side of the country road from Ipplepen on the A381 to Marldon on the outskirts of Paignton. It is one of the few houses of its type that have survived without additions which would detract from its character.

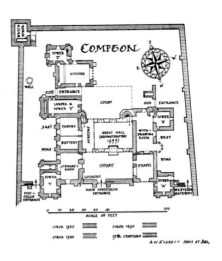

Illus 16   Compton Castle: ground floor plan

The Compton lands, part of Paignton Manor, and held by the de Compton family, passed by the marriage of Joan, co-heiress of William de Compton, to Geoffrey Gilbert early in the fourteenth century. He was the son of Thomas Gilbert of Totnes, and with only one break from 1800–1930, Compton has been the home of the family ever since.

The earliest parts of the Castle, and the nucleus around which it developed, are the great hall, 42ft × 21ft × 33ft to the roof apex, with buttery (wine store) and pantry, and solar above, dating from c 1340 (see illus 16). A little over a century later c 1450–75, the buildings at the west end of the hall were re-built, a chapel was established to the northwest of the hall, and a larger solar, watch-tower and kitchen were built. About 1520, the buildings at the east end of the hall were taken down, the buttery and pantry were reconstructed, and the wing was extended northwards to form the steward's room, and southwards for a larder and the great kitchen. Also constructed at this period were the four towers, three of them with machicolations for defence, the whole being enclosed on three sides by the court wall 24ft in height, with a watch-tower in the southeast corner.

Compton, when all this work was complete – towers, gun ports, loopholes, lookouts, and crenellated portcullis – though not impregnable, must have been strong enough for protection against the French raids which were a regular feature of the early sixteenth century, notably at Teignmouth, Plymouth and Fowey. These defences were sufficient to prevent surprise by a raiding force, and strong enough to give protection to its inhabitants, and to the animals and food supplies.

Otho Gilbert of Compton died in 1547, and his widow Katherine married Walter Raleigh of Fardell in Devon (see Boringdon Gate Piers p 133), and became the mother of Sir Walter Raleigh (1552–1618). One of his half-brothers, Humphrey (Otho's second son) was knighted in 1570, and has a claim to immortality for the decisive part he played in founding the colony of Newfoundland in August 1583; a month afterwards he was lost at sea in the *Squirrel* near the Azores. His son, Raleigh, founded Sagadahoc colony in Maine in 1607. From this Gilbert descended the late Commander Walter Raleigh Gilbert (1889–1977) who married Joan Willock. They gave the property to the Trust in 1951.

Illus 17   Principal front of Compton Castle, south Devon

When they purchased Compton in 1930, it had become a farm-house, occupied in a few rooms only in the east wing; the west wing was in ruins smothered in ivy, a veritable shambles. With the skilled professional advice of Mr A. W. Everett FSA, and their own enthusiasm, they rebuilt most of the Castle over twenty years. It was a magnificent achievement, and when they handed over the building to the Trust in 1951, only one feature was lacking. The hall was still open to the sky. It was then agreed by them and the Trust that the hall should be rebuilt and for this work they engaged Mr F. A. Key FRIBA of the then Ancient Monuments Department of the Ministry of Works, receiving much help and encouragement from friends and relations including Gilberts in America. Included in this final reconstruction was the restoration of the west wing. Today this medieval house is seen once more in splendid order, part of the historic heritage of Britain that has been preserved for posterity (see illus 17). Almost 350 acres are part of the Compton estate.

Knightshayes Court

What has so often been called 'the dreaming spires of St Pancras', but is usually called St Pancras Station, Sir George Gilbert Scott's Grand Hotel built for the Midland Railway between 1866–73 epitomises High Victorian architecture. Many architects of the period produced their own brand of the style, but none better than William Burges ARA (1827–81) whose buildings, often massive, learned and glittering, combined medieval romanticism and lavish decoration. His best known are the Cathedral Church of St Finbarr built for the Church of Ireland in Cork (1870), the reconstruction of Cardiff Castle for the 3rd Marquess of Bute (1875), and the exotic Tower House in Kensington (1876). It was Burges who received, in 1869, a commission from John Heathcoat-Amory to design a country house in northeast Devon to be called Knight-shayes Court. It is located half a mile east of the A396 Tiverton–Bampton road and $1\frac{1}{2}$ miles from Tiverton.

The Handbook for Travellers in Devon and Cornwall (1865) says

'Lace-making was introduced into Tiverton in 1816, and is now a thriving business. The factory of Messrs Heathcoat is worth a visit and employs about 1500 hands. Adjoining it is a large iron-foundry belonging to the same firm.'

The introduction to the town of this industry was due to the genius of John Heathcoat, born at Duffield in Derbyshire in August 1783. When he was twenty, he invented a bobinette lace machine, and improved and patented it in 1809. His mill in Loughborough prospered until it was wrecked in 1816 by a Luddite gang. Heathcoat then decided to leave Leicestershire; in Tiverton he found water power on the Exe for a mill and, due to a slump in agriculture and the decline in woollen and cotton industries in the town, a plentiful supply of labour. His new mill was warmly welcomed by the townsfolk and he became, after 1832, member of parliament for the town, and a great philanthropist, dying in 1861.

The company he founded was inherited by his grandson, John Heathcoat-Amory, the child of his daughter Anne who had married Samuel Amory, a London banker. The new owner followed his grandfather as Liberal MP, continued the mill, and married in 1863. Five years later he decided to build himself a new house on high ground north of the town, and the foundation stone of William Burges' mansion was laid in 1869. Progress was slow, and the architect's elaborate designs for the interior (see illus 18), for which he was famed, did not materialise until 1873. The owner chafed at the delay, and the family legend is that, on returning from a voyage abroad in 1874, the year in which he was created Sir John Heathcoat-Amory Bart, and finding that the internal wood-work was still being fitted, he lost patience and sacked the architect! He then brought in J. D. Crace, a member of a family of artist-designers whose decorations were to be seen in many country houses. Crace's decorative scheme was itself not completed until the end of the decade and, although less elaborate than Burges', it included the painted ceilings and stencilled wall-surfaces then much in vogue. As fashion changed, most of Crace's decorations were almost entirely removed or covered over, and such was the case when Sir John's grandson, Sir John the 3rd baronet, died in 1972,

leaving Knightshayes and 262 acres of land to the Trust.

A few years before his death, Sir John had vested his beautiful garden, some of it laid out by his grandfather, in a charitable trust, to which he later added the house, and provided that the whole should pass to the National Trust with an endowment.

The garden was first opened to visitors in the summer of 1974 and proved a great attraction. The south terraces are part of Burges' original landscape design, and in the 1950s and '60s Lady Amory, who now lives in the east wing, began to extend the gardens which now cover almost 25 acres. Notable features are a topiary fox and hounds on a yew hedge to the east of the house made fifty years ago, and the cedar house by the glade (1972).

When the Trust took over, fittings put in by both Burges and Crace were found in Burges' stable block, and in preparing the house for visitors (opened summer 1976), the Trust has taken the opportunity to uncover and restore Crace's decorations where there was clear evidence of their existence. Of special interest is the fact that these original decorations have been restored by the firm that carried them out nearly 100 years ago, Campbell Smith and Company of Muswell Hill, London. Founded in 1873, they started by painting and gilding Burges' designs, as at Cardiff Castle.

The contents of the house consist of family portraits, a small collection of Old Master paintings, and much of the china and furniture. The Trust has added further items, and although Knightshayes Court is not presented today as it was lived in by a family until 1973, it is a fascinating example of a mid-Victorian building (see illus 19) by a remarkable architect, little of whose domestic work has survived, with decorative detail of unusual interest. Let one example suffice – the corbel figure on the main staircase of a tortoiseshell cat, characteristic of Burges' sense of whimsy. Protruding from the tortoise shell is the cat's head!

The house and garden, which opened in 1974, attracted 23,000 visitors in 1976.

Illus 18 The hall (1873) of Knightshayes Court near Tiverton. Architect: William Burges

(*overleaf*) *Illus 19* Knightshayes Court near Tiverton from the northwest

Saltram

This noble mansion and its park of 291 acres was given to the Trust in 1957 by the Treasury, together with the more important contents of the house, in lieu of estate duty. It had accepted them from the executors of the 4th Earl of Morley. During the following twelve years a further 215 acres were added by purchase or exchange. The estate is located on the southeast branch of the estuary of the River Plym, 3 miles northeast of the centre of Plymouth. Access is off the A38 west of Plympton.

The name derives from the fact that salt was produced from salt pans on the tidal estuary, and it occurs as 'Salterham' as far back as 1218. The 'ham' also suggests a homestead on the site, long before the building in the late Tudor period of the house that forms the core of the present mansion, and which can be seen in the courtyard onto which the restaurant looks.

This late medieval house was possibly built by the Dorset family of Bagg who came to Plymouth c 1510 and who were living here in the second half of that century. The last of the Baggs, George, was banished to Barbados, and Sir George Carteret took possession in 1661. Thirty years later, the construction of what is now the central part of the west front, enlarged and adapted from the Tudor building, took place.

There was another change of ownership in Queen Anne's reign, when George Parker of North Molton purchased the house in 1712. He was the ancestor of the Earls of Morley; the 5th Earl died at Saltram in 1962, five years after the Trust took over. And so the 'Parkers of Saltram' were associated with the estate for precisely 250 years. The maintenance of this large house and its park is considerable, and the Trust receives grants from the Historic Buildings Council for England, and Plymouth City Council. There were 32,000 visitors in 1976.

George Parker's son, John, married Lady Catherine Poulett and c 1744 they started to build the south and east wings of the present mansion and enlarge the west wing, to form the largest mansion in Devon. The work was completed by 1750. Eighteen years later, their son John succeeded to the property and in that year he engaged the services of Robert Adam, the Scots architect (1728–92), to decorate the saloon and dining room, and to design the park lodges. Apart from the creation of the library between 1796 and 1819, and the linking up of the library and music room and the building of the Doric porch on the west front in 1818–20 by the Plymouth architect John Foulston (1772–1842), a pupil of Thomas Hardwick, there have been no further architectural changes of any importance (see illus 20).

The second John Parker was created Lord Boringdon in 1784, and was a close friend of the first President of the Royal Academy, Sir Joshua Reynolds, who was born in 1723 at Plymouth St Maurice next to Saltram. The stucco exterior of the house, a little severe, gives no real indication of the magnificence and beauty of what is inside. There are a total of fourteen portraits by Reynolds in the house including five in the morning room and four in the saloon.

Illus 20   Saltram, the west front

Robert Adam's grand saloon (see illus 21), for which his drawing still survives, is a major triumph of late eighteenth century interior design, with every detail right down to the door handles carried out as he planned it. The Axminster carpet was specially woven to echo the exquisite ceiling. The chimneypiece with its Sienna marble columns, the painted ceiling roundels by Joseph Rose and Antonio Zucchi, talented craftsmen often employed by Reynolds, Adam's giltwood stands to support Blue John candelabra, all contribute to the magnificence of this beautiful room. Neither is the dining room any less impressive, with its attractive curved segmental sideboard, flanked by urn-shaped wine coolers.

Another delight of this house is the Chinese dressing room and Chinese Chippendale bedroom; the wallpaper, probably dating from the reign of K'ang Hsi (1662–1722), is possibly the earliest of its kind extant in the British Isles. The contents and arrangement of the bedroom show how the exotic fashion for *chinoiserie* blends with an English country bedroom. The mahogany four-poster was supplied c 1760 from Chippendale's workshop.

John Parker and his successors provided Saltram with an appropriate setting and carefully planted the park, woods and gardens. The lime avenue, along whose verges grow narcissus varieties of the Victorian period, primroses and white and pink *Cyclamen neapolitanum*, was planted about 1820. The 'Castle' of c 1771 is a little octagon in Gothick dress with a classical interior. The orangery was begun in 1773 and completed two years later, an 'improvement' by Henry Stockman, amateur architect and fine wood-carver, of a design by 'Mr Richmond'. The orange trees were imported from Italy in 1775. The entire park at Saltram has a feeling of spaciousness with the fine trees planted mostly in the eighteenth century in the manner of Lancelot 'Capability' Brown.

On 15 August 1789, King George III and his Queen and three Princesses visited Saltram. Fanny Burney was present as Keeper of the Queen's Robes, and she recorded in her diary 'Saltram is one of the most magnificent houses in the Kingdom, its view is noble!'. It remains so to this day.

Illus 21   The grand saloon at Saltram by Robert Adam, 1768

6 The Great Houses of Cornwall

Antony House

Located off the A38 road 2 miles northwest of Torpoint, near the confluence of the River Lynher with the Hamoaze (River Tamar), Antony is one of the great houses of Cornwall and has long been associated with Cornish history. When Jane Courtenay married Sir Nicholas Carew, Antony came to her fourth son, Alexander, who died in 1492. His great-great-grandson Richard Carew, the historian, succeeded to the estate in 1564 at the age of ten and was Sheriff of Cornwall in 1586. During the last decade of the sixteenth century, or earlier, Richard compiled his masterly work *The Survey of Cornwall* printed in London 'by S. S. for John Jaggard' in 1602. His dedication is to Sir Walter Raleigh, Lieut General of Cornwall, and begins 'This mine ill-husbanded Survey, long since begun, a great while discontinued, lately reviewed and now hastily finished,' and ends 'Now your journey endeth with the land, called by the Cornish Pedn an laaz and by the English The lands end. Because we are arrived I will heere sit mee downe and rest. Deo gloria: mihi gratia. 1602. April 23.' His portrait at Antony, painted in 1586, and his book reveal a serene and contented man.

It was his great-grandson, Sir William Carew, who built Antony as it stands today. Begun in 1710, it was completed eleven years later, and the accounts are still extant to show the activities of the quarrymen, masons and carpenters, and the amounts of straw brought in for brickmaking during the years 1714–18. Sir Nikolaus

Pevsner says 'this without doubt is the best example of its date in Cornwall'.

No record has ever been found of Antony's architect, and there is no foundation at all for its attribution to James Gibbs, designer of the Radcliffe Camera in Oxford and the Senate House in Cambridge which was started in 1722. However, the composition is worthy of a better originator than the unknown Naval architect from Plymouth Dockyard who has been suggested. Suffice to say that whoever designed the house was an unusually accomplished architect.

It was built of silver-grey Pentewan stone from a quarry near Mevagissey, brought up by sea, and is entered through a forecourt flanked by mellow red-brick long pavilions with arcades and segment-headed windows at first floor level. These pavilions or wings are connected by ornamental brick walling to corner pavilions with Chinese-like pointed lead roofs that give a touch of gaiety to the whole composition. The outer pavilions are linked by a stone wall with piers and stone balls, and central wrought iron gates. The porte-cochère was added after 1838 (see illus 22).

The rooms are panelled in Dutch oak or pine, and contain many pieces contemporary with the house. Furnishings, china, books, tapestries, family relics and specially the portraits illustrate the way this family has been concerned with events in English and Cornish history. There are some pieces of English Renaissance furniture and some panelling surviving from the Tudor house which preceded the existing mansion. Specially to be noted is Edward

Illus 22   Antony, east Cornwall: the principal front

Bower's portrait (1648) of King Charles I at his trial that dominates the hall, and in the library the painting of Sir Alexander Carew who was beheaded in 1644. He was anti-Royalist and so the family hacked his portrait out of its frame and put it in the cellar. As it hangs today, the crude stitches with which it was put in again are clearly visible.

Upstairs in the corridor is a group of family portraits of the present century; particularly notable is Ellis Robert's painting of Lady Beatrice Pole-Carew, daughter of the 3rd Marquess of Ormonde, who was a veritable Irish beauty.

The present head of the family is Sir John Carew-Pole, who was High Sheriff of Cornwall in 1947–8, Chairman of the County Council 1952–63, and Lord-Lieutenant 1962–77.

Humphrey Repton was consulted about Antony, and drew up one of his 'Red Books' for both house and grounds in 1792, the same year that he landscaped the park at Port Eliot at St Germans. He proposed embellishments to the house and terrace and its approaches but they were not carried out. Had they been, much of the character of Antony would have been obscured. There are however three great vistas from the northwest front, great tree-lined avenues down to the River Lynher, and whether designed by Repton or not, they have produced a truly romantic park. At the far end of one of these vistas, three-quarters of a mile from the house on the north bank of the river, is the fine 1908 Forder granite viaduct on the GWR main line.

On the bank of the estuary to the north of the park in the wilderness is the charming Bath Pond House that may be seen by appointment. This building was designed by Thomas Parlby in October 1788 and was probably completed by 1790. Repton in his Red Book proposed a walk to this 'Cold Bath', which consists of an open-air plunge bath partially roofed after the manner of a Roman atrium. It is filled with salt water from the Lynher via a quarry pool and sluice. There is an attractive panelled changing room. It was repaired and endowed with money given by Miss Maisie Radford of St Antony-in-Roseland in memory of her sister Evelyn.

Antony was given to the Trust in 1961 with 29 acres, since

Illus 23 Cotehele: the southeast front

extended to 63 acres, by Sir John who still lives in the house. As the house is still occupied all visitors to the building are shown over it by conducted tours only.

Cotehele House

Sir John Betjeman has written of the large parish of Calstock, wherein Cotehele is to be found, 'orchard slopes looking across to the woodlands of the Devon banks of the Tamar, the lanes down to them steep and narrow between mossy stones of the hedges. Let he who loves Cornwall and can read a 1in ordnance map find them for himself.' Several of these delightful lanes will lead the visitor to Cotehele, but a different and quite fascinating way is by railway from Plymouth, northwards up the east bank of the Tamar, over the viaduct into Cornwall and alighting at Calstock Station. Walk down to the river bank, along the old quay past Danescombe Hotel and enter the garden of Cotehele at the northeast corner.

At once the visitor is in a garden of medieval Cornwall, and quite soon the highly romantic house is discovered, one of the most authentic surviving examples of a knightly dwelling built in the late medieval tradition (see illus 23).

85

Hilaria de Cotehele was the heiress who in 1353 brought the manor in marriage to William Edgcumbe, son of Richard Edgcumbe of Milton Abbot in Devon, 7 miles to the northwest. Their house was a compact stone building, parts of which still survive in the present house. In due course it was inherited by Richard Edgcumbe MP for Tavistock in 1468. This Richard declared against the Crown in 1485 and was pursued by Richard III's agent, Sir Henry Trenowth of Bodrugan, only escaping from Cotehele with his life by means of a trick. Richard Carew relates the story in his *Survey of Cornwall*

'hee was hotly pursued and narrowly searched for. Which extremity taught him a sudden policy, to put a stone in his cap, and tumble the same into the water[River Tamar], while these rangers were fast at his heeles, who looking downe after the noyse, and seeing his cap swimming thereon, supposed that he had desperately drowned himselfe, gave over their farther hunting, and left him liberty to shift away and shipt over into Brittanie: For a grateful remembrance of which delivery, hee afterwards builded a Chappell'.

This small building 70ft above the river, the 'Chapel on the Cliff', is still extant, restored in 1620 and again in 1769. It was dedicated to SS George and Thomas à Becket.

Trenowth was nothing better than a common marauder and bandit, and a just nemesis overcame him. In turn, he leapt from a rock and into a ship for France, at Bodrugan's Leap, also Trust property (see page 52).

Richard joined forces with Henry Tudor, fought at Bosworth in 1485, and returned to Cotehele, rewarded for his loyalty by Henry VII with a knighthood and appointment as Ambassador to Scotland. He supervised the enlargements to the old house, building the present entrance gateway and gate tower, the barn, an upper floor around the inner court and the chapel. He died at Morlaix in Brittany in 1489, and was succeeded by his son, Piers, who was knighted by Henry VIII. Piers' marriage to Joan Durnford, who was wealthy, enabled him to complete the extensions started by his father. They were completed by 1539 and his finest achievement is Cotehele great hall, finished before 1520. No further additions were made until 1627 when the northwest tower, said to have been

Illus 24   Cotehele: ground floor plan

built by Sir Thomas Cotehele, was added (see illus 24). Sir Thomas, a shadowy figure, was a Dutchman who had fled from the appalling persecutions carried out in the Netherlands by the Duke of Alva. He had no connexion with the old Cotehele family, but married his daughter to a later Sir Richard Edgcumbe. He is, however, supposed to have lived at Cotehele for a long period.

It was Sir Richard Edgcumbe who built the new house for the family at Mount Edgcumbe between 1547–54, and towards the end of the seventeenth century the family practically ceased to live at Cotehele, which ever since has only been occupied periodically. The house by the Tamar was left much to itself, but because it was properly cared for, the Tudor buildings remained unaltered and Cotehele acquired the serenity that is so marked to this day. Its rare collection of late Stuart and early Georgian furniture has never left it.

When Mount Edgcumbe was destroyed by Nazi incendiary bombs in March 1941, the 5th Earl of Mount Edgcumbe (the earldom was conferred upon George Edgcumbe, Admiral of the Blue, in 1789) moved to Cotehele. He died in 1944, and the 6th Earl upon succeeding to the family estates suggested to the Treasury that the Cotehele property of 1287 acres should be accepted in part payment of estate duty and handed over to the Trust. When this happened in 1947, Cotehele was the first historic country house and estate to be acquired in this way. The Trust is indeed indebted to the Treasury and to the 6th Earl for such a valuable precedent. When he died in 1965, the family trustees generously continued to leave on loan in the state rooms all the tapestries, armour and furniture. Nine years later, these contents became Trust property via the Treasury who had accepted them in lieu of estate duty. The great estate, two square miles of it, is an agriculatural estate without special access for the public, and includes the entire village of Bohetherick to the South.

The great hall of c 1515, one of the most impressive in the West Country, is unusual in that it never seems to have had screens in the normal medieval fashion. The fine roof is kept taut and is decorated with moulded braces, a technique used in earlier times. This is the visitor's entrèe into the house, and at once the note of Tudor tradition, present throughout the whole building, is struck. Most of the rooms are hung from floor to ceiling with seventeenth century tapestries.

In the southwest corner of the old dining room, a flight of narrow steps leads through the wall into the chapel, probably dedicated to the same two saints as the church of Luxulyan near St Blazey in Cornwall, SS Cyricus (sometimes Quiricus) and Julitta. It was licensed in 1411, and behind the altar is a Flemish triptych of the Adoration of the Magi. The altar frontal is a beautiful piece of appliqué work, silver on purple, with the arms of Sir Piers Edgcumbe and the twelve Apostles. On the north wall is a copy of the monument to Sir Richard (1489) at Morlaix. This beautiful chapel has a little bellcote with pinnacles, looking like a holy well building, and when it was all complete c 1487, Sir Richard installed a clock. This survives, the earliest clock in Britain still unaltered and in its original position.

The gardens of Cotehele completely suit this medieval house, a tapestry of stone walls, terraces, hedges, trees and water. West of the northwest tower is a touching dog gravestone up against a wall 'TO YARROW: My good and faithful companion 1876–91'. Ancient sycamores flank the approach alongside the barn (c 1500), in which there is an excellently run restaurant. There are many exotic trees, notably the golden ash, the 'handkerchief' tree *Davidia involucrata*, large magnolias, a liriodendron – the tulip tree, and other sub-tropical features of a Cornish garden, bamboos, palms, azaleas and eucryphias. Worthy of note is the medieval dovecote, looking for all the world like a giant stone preserve jar!

To the north of the garden is the 'Prospect Tower', 60ft high, roofless and now hollow, triangular in plan. Was it built in 1789 with the advancement of Lord Mount Edgcumbe to an earldom, perhaps being used to send messages by heliograph from his house at Mount Edgcumbe to Cotehele, a distance of 10 miles?

This beautiful house is so popular that 43,000 visitors came to see it in 1976. A splendid innovation is the film room where there is a continuous programme of transparencies of Cotehele scenes lithographed c 1840 by Nicholas Condy contrasted with those of the present day.

For details of the mill and quay see Chapter 10.

Lanhydrock House

The parish of Lanhydrock was one of the oldest possessions of the Monastery of St Petroc in Bodmin, which was perhaps founded by St Petroc in the sixth century. Since the Cure of Souls was served by a chaplain appointed by the prior, without any reference to the bishop, it was a peculiar that became a donative on the Dissolution in 1538. The Priory grange next to the church was obtained by the Glynn family of Glynn (nearby) but shortly afterwards passed by marriage to another family, the Lyttletons. Their heiress brought it on marriage to Thomas Trenance of Withiel and his son sold it in 1620 to Sir Richard Robartes, born Roberts, a wealthy merchant banker of Truro. James I created him Baron

Illus 25   Lanhydrock House near Bodmin: the north wing (1642) the gatehouse (1651) and formal garden

Robartes in 1624 – for £10,000! – and it was he who started to build his new house to replace the old grange at about this time. He died in 1634 and his son John completed it by 1642. John started building the delightful gatehouse in 1636 but did not finish it until 1651 (see illus 25).

John, the 2nd Baron, became Lord-Lieutenant of Cornwall, declared for Cromwell, garrisoned Lanhydrock, and fought at Edge-hill. At the Restoration, he was 'received into favour' and died in 1685. This family estate subsequently descended to the 1st Viscount Clifden, Charles Agar, whose son Thomas Agar-Robartes was created Baron Robartes of Lanhydrock and Truro in 1869. His marriage to Juliana Pole-Carew of Antony in 1839 forged a link between two great families, both of whose houses are now cared for by the Trust.

For over forty years, Lord and Lady Robartes lived at Lanhydrock, their benevolence and philanthropy coupled with a patrician authority over their substantial estate. Much of their wealth came from mineral dues when Cornwall was one of the richest mining areas in Europe, but, unlike so many others of his time, Lord Robartes was never a rapacious landlord. In bad times, dues were remitted and other employment was found for miners. His care for people culminated in his building the Miners' Hospital in Redruth between 1863–71. He rebuilt his farms and cottages to a high standard, supported the building of Cornish railways, planted the woodland that now makes such a splendid feature in the Fowey

Valley, and in 1857 employed George Gilbert Scott to enlarge the house and lay out formal gardens. All in all, the 1st Baron was an enlightened Victorian landowner.

The Carolean house that Sir Richard Robartes started to build was originally constructed around an open quadrangle, the later gatehouse joined by flanking walls enclosing a forecourt. The east

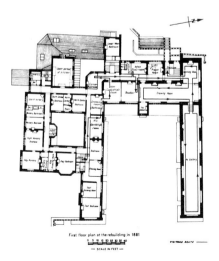

Illus 26   Lanhydrock House: ground floor plan at the rebuilding in 1881

Illus 27   Lanhydrock House: first floor plan at the rebuilding in 1881

91

wing was pulled down about 1780 thus giving the house its present plan. The forecourt walls were removed and Scott's improvement in the late 1850s created the terraces and formal flower beds that now form the setting of the house. He also added the coach house, stables and grooms' quarters. The design was entrusted to an assistant, a Cornishman from Liskeard, Richard Coad, and the work was complete by 1860.

Disaster struck when the kitchen chimney caught fire during a gale on 4 April 1881, and the house was almost gutted, only the north wing and the entrance porch remaining. Coad was by then in practice on his own account in London, and Lord Robartes commissioned him to carry out the reconstruction which was finished by 1885. The rebuilding was done to the original plan, and several of the principal rooms, notably the smoking room and the billiards room, have a Victorian charm and are particularly evocative of a recent but now vanished age (see illus 26 and 27).

Specially interesting is the great room of the house, the gallery in the north wing untouched by the fire. It is 116ft long, with tall mullioned windows letting in the sunlight on the south wall. It has a shallow tunnel-vault plaster ceiling filled with twenty-four panels showing incidents from the Old Testament from the Creation to the burial of Isaac. The main panels are surrounded by smaller ones with a multitude of birds and beasts, and the work is almost certainly attributable to Devonshire plasterers, the Abbots of Frithelstock near Bideford.

Illus 28 Lanhydrock House: the great kitchen. Architect: Richard Coad, 1885

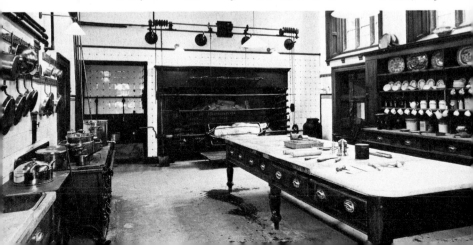

None the less interesting are the kitchen quarters, built after the fire to provide high standards of cuisine. The great kitchen is the pièce de resistance (see illus 28) whilst around it are the dairy and its scullery, the game, fish and meat larders, the bakehouse and main scullery, not forgetting the lamp room and gun room, wine cellar and china closet. Robert Kerr, the architect who designed Bearwood in Berkshire for John Walter III, proprietor of *The Times*, at a cost in 1865–74 of £250,000, wrote in his book *The Gentleman's House* that with an income of £40,000 a year, up to thirty indoor and thirty outdoor servants were needed. The domestic offices at Lanhydrock are a reminder of the size of a wealthy Victorian household.

This house, located in a beautiful part of Cornwall, was given to the Trust with 442 acres of park and woodland by the 7th Viscount Clifden in 1953, and the acreage has since been extended to 741. Protected by beechwoods, and the famous avenue of beeches and sycamores, some planted as long ago as 1648, the whole is a jewel in the Cornish landscape with a fine prospect to the east to the 532ft summit of Bofarnel Downs. The formal garden contains several bronze urns by Louis Ballin, goldsmith to Louis XIV, which were originally in the Château de Bagatelle in Paris, built for Marie Antoinette. The 7th Viscount Clifden purchased them in Gloucestershire and brought them to Lanhydrock. The collection of trees here was started even before 1634, but Lord Clifden created the informal plantings from 1930 onwards. There are many large magnolias, particularly the exotic *M. campbellii*, azaleas and rhododendrons, tulip trees, swamp cypress, and recent planting of hydrangeas and summer flowering shrubs.

The popularity of Lanhydrock is shown by its 52,000 visitors during 1976 and it is located $1\frac{1}{2}$ miles due west of Bodmin Road Station and off the A38.

St Michael's Mount

Majestic Michael rises – he whose brow
Is crowned with castles, and whose rocky sides
Are clad with dusky ivy; he whose base,

Beat by the storms of ages, stands unmoved
Amidst the wreck of things – the change of time,
That base, encircled by the azure waves
Was once with verdure clad; the towering oaks,
Whose awful shades among the Druids strayed
To cut the hallowed mistletoe, and hold
High converse with their gods.

Sir Humphry Davy FRS (born Penzance 1778)

A diary called *The Pocket Magnet* was published in London in 1813 for Peacock and Bampton of Salisbury Square. It contained a small engraving of St Michael's Mount and some notes of its history

On record as a place of pilgrimage in the fifth century: Edward the Confessor founded a Benedictine Priory and William I made it a cell to Mont St Michel: Edward IV gave it to Syon Nunnery: Granted to Humphrey Arundel in 1538 and subsequently to John St Aubyn: In 1700, only one house and the castle but now (1813) greatly improved: a busy port in the pilchard season: eighty houses erected and the fish cellars.

That, in the smallest compass, is the history of this island which is perhaps more evocative of Cornwall than any other place.

The Cornish called it *Carrek Los yn Cos*, 'the Grey Rock in the Wood', and at times of very low water, the remains of old trees are still to be seen in the sands of Mounts Bay, and were photographed as recently as February 1974. Recent scientific analysis has indicated that the trees were growing about 1800BC, and the stone of the Mount is grey granite. For centuries, the legend has persisted that St Michael, patron saint of Cornwall, appeared to fishermen on the Mount in the year 495, and gave it its name. Precisely the same legend appertains to Mont St Michel where St Michael appeared to St Aubert in the year 710, and where Richard, Duke of Normandy, founded a Benedictine Abbey whose great church was completed in 1136.

The Celtic church was very much in evidence in Cornwall after the withdrawal of the Romans, and there is an early tradition that

St Cadoc, founder of the Welsh monastery of Llancarvan in Glamorgan, visited the Mount during the sixth century, and that St Keyne, whose Well is found near Liskeard, came on a pilgrimage to the Mount. High on the northeastern corner of the island is a Celtic cross that has probably stood on this site for a thousand years, and there is another on the south side. The Domesday Book (1086) records that in the time of Edward the Confessor the Mount was held by Brismar the Priest.

The recorded history of the Mount begins in 1135 with the establishment of the Benedictine Priory by Bernard, Abbot of Mont St Michel, a fact discovered in the records of the Priory of Otterton, a small Benedictine house near Budleigh Salterton. The Priory on the Mount was 'alien' owing allegiance to Mont St Michel, and so was always suspect during the 150 years after 1260 when England was continually at war with France. The crunch finally came in 1414 when Henry V's parliament 'decreed that all alien priories should be suppressed to the intent that English monies should not help the enemy'. And so the Benedictine tenure ended after almost 380 years.

Henry V's favourite order of nuns was the Brigittines; he founded their great house of Syon Abbey in Middlesex in 1415. He also gave them the alien Priory at Otterton after the expulsion of the Benedictines there. St Michael's Mount had long been the most famous and rich of all the Cornish places of pilgrimage, and there is some evidence that Henry had intended it to go to the Abbess of Syon, but he died in 1422.

She petitioned the new king, Henry VI, to confirm the grant, and he did so in a Charter of 1424, and from that date there is further evidence that the grant was made to trustees so that Syon did not take possession until 1437. On his visitation to the Mount in 1425, the Diocesan found there had been only three monks in residence, the remnant of the Benedictines. He decided that for the future there should be three chaplains, the chief to be called the 'Arch-Priest', a title still used in the Orthodox Church. The first Arch-Priest was William Morton, who started to build the first harbour wall in 1427, at which time a Charter was granted to enable tolls to be levied on ships. This harbour wall must be the long 480ft western pier built with huge unwrought blocks of stone, similar to those used on the harbour wall at Mousehole, started by the Mount Benedictines in 1393.

In July 1437, Joan, Abbess of Syon, took possession of the Mount but not for long. Henry VI was looking for an endowment for his new foundations at Cambridge and Eton; so parliament evicted Syon and, surprise, condemned the Abbess to pay damages for trespass! Joan was succeeded by Elizabeth Muston as Abbess of Syon and Edward IV granted her full restoration in November 1461 and confirmed it in a Charter the following February. The Abbey, then built the new Lady Chapel to the northeast of the main church in the following year, and the Abbess appointed a person of high rank in Cornwall to act as receiver (accountant). In view of later history, it is interesting that a Peter St Aubyn was the holder of this office in 1514. At the suppression of all the religious houses the last Arch-Priest of the Mount was John Arscott. He became vicar of St Clement near Truro in 1537, and schoolmaster at Penryn for £10 per annum.

In 1539, the King appointed Humphrey Arundell as Mount Governor. Ten years later, he lead the Cornish rising against the new Prayer Book, and was subsequently hanged at Tyburn. If the Prayer Book had been translated into Cornish, as it was into Welsh and Irish, things might have been different!

During the fifty years from 1550 to 1600, the Mount was on Crown Lease to the Milliton family of Pengersick Castle, Praa Sands (the Trust were granted a covenant over its remains in 1968) and then to Arthur Harris as Governor in 1596. By then the Treasury was getting low in funds after numerous wars, and the Crown sold the island to two 'dealers in church lands', Messrs Bellot and Burden. They in turn passed it to Sir Robert Cecil, later Earl of Salisbury, whose title was confirmed in 1612. In 1640, Salisbury sold to Sir Francis Basset and his son Sir Arthur sold to Colonel John St Aubyn in 1659. The St Aubyns have been there ever since, and the 3rd Lord St Levan (the peerage was granted in 1887) gave this historic place to the Trust in 1954. It had become clear by that time that higher and higher taxation and increasing costs would sooner or later make it difficult to meet the expenses of maintenance. It was a question of whether to commercialise the island as the French have done with Mont St Michel since it was 'taken over' by the Government late in the nineteenth century, or to hand over to the Trust. The latter course was taken, subject to a lease of part of the castle to the family, and today it is lived in by the Hon John St Aubyn and his wife, Susan.

The Reverend Rory Fletcher MRCS, surgeon at Charing Cross Hospital and a canon of the Roman Catholic Cathedral of Southwark, whose history of the Mount was published in 1951, wrote: 'It does not require much imagination to realise what the erection of this church and priory must have cost their twelfth-century builders in toil and perserverance. It was a gigantic grappling with all sorts of elements, an inspiration to the beholder!' To that can be added the toil of rebuilding the church in the fourteenth century after the earthquake in September 1275, the Lady Chapel in the fifteenth, the harbour over successive periods between 1427 and 1824, the massive southeast wing during 1873–8, and the northwest staff wing in 1927.

The Blue Drawing Rooms are a fascinating example of 'Strawberry Hill Gothick', delightful chambers with stucco vaults and pretty fireplaces. At about the time they were made in the 1750s in what were then the ruins of the fifteenth century Lady Chapel, the 2nd Viscount Bateman built in the garden of Shobdon Court, Herefordshire, a fascinating Rococco-Gothic church on the site of a Norman church. Bateman's nephew, the Hon Richard Bateman, was a close friend of Horace Walpole on whose Committee of Taste the architect Richard Bentley served. It is certainly possible but not recorded that Bentley designed Shobdon. There are many similarities of detail between this church and the Blue Drawing Rooms on the Mount, and since it has recently been ascertained by John St Aubyn that Lord Bateman was in charge of a naval squadron at Falmouth in the 1750s, it is perfectly possible that he introduced the then Sir John St Aubyn to Bentley for his new Gothick alterations at the Mount (see illus 29).

97

The second son of Sir John the 5th Baronet was Robert, born at the Mount in 1786. His son Piers was born in 1815 while he was Vicar of Powick in Worcestershire. Piers became an architect, being made a Fellow of the RIBA in 1856. In 1873, Piers designed the massive southeast wing at the Mount for his cousin, later the 1st Lord St Levan. This is without question his finest work, rising sheer out of the rock, the living rooms on the top floor and three bedroom floors below. The whole is built of local granite, and the five years it took to complete provided employment for masons and other workers who had fallen on extremely hard times because of the collapse of the Cornish mining industry after 1870. It is built in granite both outside and inside, like Castle Drogo, and is a magnificent example of Victorian architecture (see illus 30).

There is a fascinating railway at the Mount, constructed about 1900. It starts at the south harbour wall, runs level for a short distance but begins to climb at gradients of 1 in 14, 1 in 4, and 1 in 1¾ for the final 120ft to the summit, which is 650ft from the harbour. Most of it was made by blasting a deep trench, laying the track, brick-arching over and then covering with soil, but the final section is through a very steep tunnel cut through the granite at an angle of 30 degrees. At the foot is a Crompton Parkinson electric winding engine, the cable rising overhead through the tunnel and pulling up a single four-wheeled wagon. This wagon has so far travelled about 23,000 miles, carrying all sorts, from dustbins to his lordship's coronation robes!

This famous place is always attractive particularly when seen in silhouette (see illus 31) or in the winter when a great southwest gale is pounding huge waves on the rocks. Sometimes Mounts Bay is wreathed in sea mist, with the castle floating like a ghost on cotton wool.

Pilgrims came here perhaps over a thousand years ago. They still come to pray in its ancient and beautiful church, restored for choral worship in 1811, or to wonder at its history. During 1976,

Illus 29   St Michael's Mount: the blue drawing room c 1755

there were 121,000 visitors, and the record achieved for one day was 3,300. The stone causeway is normally open for visitors on foot two hours before and after low water: there are ferries at other times.

Trerice

This beautiful late Tudor house is found in a narrow lane a mile southwest of the A3058 at Kestle Mill: the road from Summercourt (on the A30) that leads to Newquay. It is in the parish of St Newlyn East and $1\frac{1}{2}$ miles northeast of that village. The narrow lane, winding between high Cornish hedges, leads the visitor to the house, which is situated in a little valley, and has undergone little alteration in the four centuries since it was built. Through the valley runs a stream that flows into the Gannel, indeed the very name Trerice derives from the Cornish *Tre-res*, the house by the ford.

The Cornish family of Arundell obtained the estate in the time of Edward III when Ralph married Jane Trerise, and they held it for the next four hundred years. In 1471, Sir John Arundell was ordered by Edward IV to relieve St Michael's Mount, which had been seized by the Earl of Oxford, and there he was killed. It was his great-grandson, the 4th Sir John, who built Trerice in 1572–3. He married first Katherine Coswarth of the nearby village of Colan; her great-uncle, John Coswarth, was engaged in rebuilding

(left) Illus 30   The southeast wing of St Michael's Mount designed by Piers St Aubyn and built 1873–8. The roof of the porch is covered with hand-made interlocking granite tiles

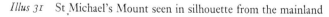

Illus 31   St Michael's Mount seen in silhouette from the mainland

his house there about 1570. Katherine probably encouraged her husband to do the same, and the work was completed in 1573, the year before Sir John became High Sheriff of Cornwall. Their eldest daughter Juliana married, at the age of 14, the Cornish historian Richard Carew of Antony (see page 82).

The 6th Sir John distinguished himself at Edgehill and was created Baron Arundell of Trerice in 1664; the Patent creating this barony came to light at a London booksellers in 1953. It was purchased by the Trust and now adorns the wall of the screens passage in the house. His son, the seventh John and 2nd Baron, married Margaret, heiress of Sir John Acland of Broadclyst in Devon, and Trerice subsequently descended to the Acland estates. The Aclands held the property until 1915, and soon afterwards the house and its manor farm of 500 acres was bought by Cornwall County Council. They in turn sold the house, which changed hands several times before being acquired by the Trust in 1953, when once again it was reunited with the Acland estate which had been given to the Trust ten years before by Sir Richard Acland.

Trerice faces east and is seen across a turfed forecourt set between high stone walls. Its facade is E-shaped, and projecting from the roof are five beautiful curved gables with scrolled finials, three of one pattern, and two of another. They are very like the gables of the same period that crown the facades of the merchants' houses along the canals in Amsterdam. Perhaps Sir John's service as a soldier in the Netherlands encouraged him to use this form of decoration, even to secure the services of a Dutch architect fleeing from the abominable rule of the Duke of Alva then at its worst (1572). Many Dutch refugees fled to Britain at that time.

The principal facade of the house is faced in a hard Cornish stone called elvan or 'growan', and the bay to the south of the porch is wholly given over to a magnificent window, mullioned and transomed, in twenty-four lights containing 576 panes of glass, much of it original. The controversial decision to test 'Concorde' aircraft over Cornwall several years ago caused considerable damage to some of this priceless Tudor glazing.

That part of the building to the north of the porch had become

Illus 32 Trerice: the principal front as it appeared in 1912

so dilapidated by the middle of the nineteenth century that in 1860 its two gables were removed, the roof taken off, and the window openings blocked up (see illus 32).

After the Trust took over, using a grant from the Historic Buildings Council and other money, this northern part of the building was completely restored. By sheer good fortune, the carved stonework of the gables had been stored and so once again they were re-instated, and the whole building re-roofed in Delabole slate (see illus 33).

The south front is quite different but equally charming, with its semi-circular bay rising through two storeys, its 'dunce-cap' roof having a large lead ball finial. The windows on the first floor of this bay light the solar. Sash windows on this elevation were inserted later but do not detract from the informal character of the whole.

Inside, the house is arranged on the medieval plan with a screens passage entered from the porch, and great hall beyond, 36ft × 22ft

(*overleaf*) *Illus 33* The restored principal front of Trerice

with a flat ceiling, contemporary with the house, plastered and moulded with medallions, strapwork and pendants. The fireplace, its scrolled plaster overmantel supported by caryatids, bears the date 1572. The 20ft long table, constructed of oak from the Acland estate in Somerset, is about 150 years old.

The library had been divided into two rooms, but it was restored to its orginal size in 1969, and it contains many interesting pieces of furniture. Of particular note is the armchair fitted with an adjustable lectern that belonged to Thomas Clarkson of Wisbech, an associate of Wilberforce, and a fighter for just causes as was Octavia Hill, one of the Trust's founders who also came from Wisbech.

The Tudor solar has long been called the drawing room, and it is flooded with light from the great bay window. The elaborate barrel-vaulted ceiling and frieze has even more elaborate plaster-work than the great hall, and above the frieze at the west end are the arms of Henry Fitz Alan, 24th Earl of Arundel who married Mary, daughter of Sir John, the builder of the house. Such a splendid marriage could not go unrecorded.

In the lobby at the foot of the stone spiral stairs from the musicians' gallery there is a yellow flag embroidered with a Cornish chough (a member of the crow family). During the hot summer of 1940, when a Nazi invasion was threatened, the local Defence Volunteers mustered at Trerice and paraded there, just as their ancestors had done when Napoleon threatened. They grew into a renowned battalion called 'The Cornish Choughs', and their Colour, given by the owner of the house in 1940, Charles Shepherd, was handed back to him after the war, and taken by him to Bermuda. He returned it to Trerice in 1970.

To the west of the house is a splendid and very large barn, recently restored by the Trust, whilst to the south the lawn has been planted with fruit trees, set out in the quincunx pattern used in the seventeenth century. Every tree is in line with its neighbours from whichever direction it is viewed. This beautiful house attracted 25,000 visitors in 1976 and is $1\frac{1}{2}$ miles from the railway station at Quintrell Downs on the Newquay Branch.

7 Inland Landscape of Devon

Bridford Wood and St Thomas Cleave Wood

In the Teign Valley near Dunsford, 5 miles downstream from Castle Drogo, is a lovely wooded area that the Trust acquired between 1968–76. It lies on the north and south sides of the B3212 Moreton-hampstead–Exeter road, and just inside the boundary of the Dartmoor National Park, near Steps Bridge. Bridford Wood consists of 131 acres of oak-covered hillside; not only does it provide part of the backdrop of the view across the Teign from the bridge but it also affords picnic places and over a mile of woodland walks.

St Thomas Cleave Wood is 108 acres of oak coppice sloping steeply to the stream that runs northeast from Doccombe to join the River Teign half a mile west of Steps Bridge. This is a dramatic hanging wood, best seen from the B3212 road.

Close to the bridge on the south side of the road, and forming an enclave in Bridford Wood, the Ivywood Tea Gardens had been long established but had become derelict, and planning permission existed for the inevitable bungalow. This site of one acre was purchased by the Trust, with a grant from Devon County Council, the site was then cleared, and an open glade provided for picnics.

Coombe Wood: Coombe Raleigh

A lane runs northwestwards from the centre of Honiton to the pretty village of Coombe Raleigh. The road runs underneath the by-pass, across the river Ottery and then twists sharp right and left. In this dog-leg is an attractive wood of 18 acres near Woodhayne Farm, given to the Trust in 1964.

Dunsland near Cookbury

The A3072 links Hatherleigh in northwest Devon with the market town of Holsworthy. 4 miles east of the town is Dunsland Cross, where the B3218 road led the traveller to the lonely LSWR railway station of that name where the *Atlantic Coast Express* could be boarded until 1964. At the cross, a lane runs due north to the site of Dunsland House, half a mile south of Cookbury Church. This house, of Tudor origin, enlarged in the seventeenth century, had descended by inheritance from 1066 until 1947. In 1862 it was described as 'an ancient seat', the property of W. B. Coham.

The Trust purchased the property in 1954 with 92 acres, and it was of sufficient national importance, historically and architecturally, to attract a substantial grant from the Historic Buildings Council. The restoration had just been completed when, on 18 November 1967, an appalling fire reduced it to ashes. Complete demolition was the only solution, and a memorial tablet now marks the site. The granary is now at Arlington Court (qv).

There is a site for touring caravans in the wood leased by the Trust to the Caravan Club.

Goodameavy

Five miles up the valley of the Plym from the point where its water enters the long estuary opposite Saltram is the confluence of the Plym with the Meavy at Shaugh Bridge. Here two gorges meet under a thick canopy of oak, and between the two rivers is the towering Dewerstone Rock, on which there are the remains of an Iron Age promontory fort. In *The Handbook for Travellers* (1865) it is thus described: 'this whimsical rock which rises from the bank in the shape of a pillar, surmounted by a rude capital, is now [1862] alas being converted into a quarry, the result of a new railway'. Alas, the railway was closed in 1962! Here small boys are given their first taste of mountaineering, clambering up with ropes.

395 acres were purchased or were given to the Trust in 1960, including Dewerstone and Cadworthy woods, part of Wigford Down, two farms, and fishing rights in the two rivers. There are views and walks in the National Park here, with free public access to the moor and the woods, but not to the farm land.

Hembury Woods

From the A38 at Dart Bridge, 2 miles southwest of Ashburton, turn northwest past Buckfast Abbey, and follow the lane to the west and then north until the Trust sign Hembury Woods is reached. The Trust's car park is in the wood at grid reference 730680 on sheet 188 of the 1in Ordnance Survey maps. These fine woodlands, 374 acres in total, were acquired between 1947–60, and they lie on the west side of the River Dart. Woodland rides lead through young oak woods and coppice to riverside scenery, as well as open heath of gorse and bracken. To reach the river, take the path into the wood opposite the car park on the right hand side of the lane where there is a Trust sign 'To the River'. Follow the ride in and then branch right at forestry post 2. This path leads down to the Dart, with silvery rapids and deep pools, all very idyllic on a summer day. The summit is at 500ft and on it is Hembury Castle, an Iron Age hill-fort, well planned and surrounded by three ramparts, and the remains of the motte and bailey Dane's Castle. There are fine views over the Vale of Otter. This monument has occasionally been called Hembury Fort in guide books, but should not be confused with the Fort of that name, another similar site 3 miles northwest of Honiton on the A373.

There is a fascinating $1\frac{1}{2}$ mile walk through these woods described in detail in the Country Walks booklet. Note in particular the adit in the river side, a horizontal gallery excavated by miners for copper working, and upstream the mound marking the site of the Queen of Dart mine, that in 1856 sold 174 tons of copper ore for 67s a ton.

Hentor Trowlesworthy and Willings Walls Warrens

Lying 3½ miles north and northwest of Cornwood between the Blacka Brook and Great Gnats' Head is a magnificent sweep of Dartmoor 4 miles long and covering 3333 acres. It was bought by or was given to the Trust in 1966–9 and forms part of the Plym estate. Here, where ponies graze, and the tor-outcrops on the horizon are the only features of a grey-green landscape, wholly within the Dartmoor National Park, are the remains of once flourishing settlements. In this open moorland, accessible only on foot or on the back of a horse, there is only one house, the lonely farm at Trowlesworthy Warren. There are an astonishing number of Bronze Age monuments; no less than twenty of them are shown on the small scale 1 : 50,000 Ordnance Survey map, variously marked 'Enclosures and Hut Circles', 'Cists', 'Cairns', and 'Stone Circles'. They are reminders of a centre of civilization in the pre-Christian era. Man developed this site between 15000 and 3500BC. Across to the northwest there is a splendid view over Ringmoor Down to Sheepstor, and northwards towards Princetown; the southwest boundary of the property runs across the summit of Shell Top at 1557ft. The northeast tip of the Trust's land is at Plym Head, the source of the river on the 1500ft contour.

The Plymouth born poet Noel Carrington (1777–1830) who loved this place wrote 'A holy peace pervades this moorland solitude'. He wrote much about Dartmoor, and *The Handbook for Travellers* recorded in 1865 that 'on one of the flat blocks on the ground above the Dewerstone rock is engraved his name and the date of his death, 2 September 1830.'

There is an excellent walk of 2 miles, starting at Blacka Brook bridge on the Cornwood–Yelverton road, and extending to Little Trowlesworthy Tor, fully described in the Country Walks booklet.

Holne Woods

3½ miles northwest of Ashburton is the Dart Gorge running northwest from New Bridge (a medieval structure) on the A384 up to Dartmeet. It has been a popular place for tourists for well over a century, and they were exhorted to find their way along the river bank to appreciate the magnificent scenery. In 1957, 165 acres of woodland, mainly natural oak, were given by an anonymous donor to the Trust. They extend on the east and west banks of the river upstream from New Bridge for 2½ miles, and paths run high above the river as well as along the banks.

Killerton

Lying on both sides of the M5 motorway, 7 miles northeast of Exeter, is the huge Trust estate of Killerton covering in all 6388 acres, mostly given by Sir Richard Acland Bt in 1942–3; part was also acquired from his Trustees in 1944. It includes most of the villages of Broadclyst and Budlake, and the hamlets of Westwood and Beare, and it lies between the valleys of the Clyst and Culm rivers.

The woods, extending to just over a thousand acres, are in three separate blocks; Ashclyst Forest (600 acres), and White Down and Paradise Copses lie to the southeast of the M5 motorway, and occupy the tops of two low hills; the other woods are grouped around Killerton Park to the northwest of the M5. Within the park, which covers 300 acres, is the famous Killerton Garden covering 15 acres, an exceptionally sheltered site in which there is a fine and extensive collection of trees and shrubs. Throughout the year, there is always a display of flowers or foliage.

Originating in the twelfth century at Acland Barton in North Devon, the Aclands came south to the Exeter district in the reign of Queen Elizabeth I and settled at Columbjohn, a house about a mile west of the present Killerton House on the River Culm, built c 1590. Only the gate arch, and the old chapel (restored c 1840) remain of this house. The family prospered during the eighteenth century and in the 1770s Sir Thomas Acland, 7th Baronet, had a new house designed for him by Essex architect John Johnson. This was finished by December 1779. In 1770, Sir Thomas had sent for John Veitch, a young Scot from Edinburgh who had come to London to seek his fortune, to lay out a park for the proposed new house. Veitch was then helped to establish a nursery of his own that later developed into a famous concern, and as agent to the estate he appreciated the character of the site and was able to design a landscape for it sympathetically. Apart from the initial work, little development of the garden occurred until 1808, when the 10th baronet, another Sir Thomas who died in 1871, embarked upon more ambitious plans. Veitch, who by now had earned a countrywide reputation as a landscapist, played a full part in these plans, and survivors of his planting, notably the largest beeches in the Beech Walk, exist to this day. This baronet, known to the family as the 'Great' Sir Thomas, took an immense pride in the garden which he helped to create, and lived long to enjoy it for he was eighty-three when he died.

Killerton Garden which was made on a hill has an acid soil, suiting rhododendrons and conifers, of which many species were procured from all over the world by successive baronets. On this soil, care and climate have, over 170 years, created a great arboretum. Rarely have the imagination and skill of the arboriculturist used natural landscape to more satisfying purpose.

To the northeast of the house is the Chapel of the Holy Evangelists, designed in 1837 by Professor C. R. Cockerell (1788–1863) in the neo-Norman style, then much in vogue. It was consecrated appropriately on St Matthew's Day, 21 September 1841, and is now part of the parish of Broadclyst. Its internal arrangement is that of a college chapel. Note the carved nests at each side of the west rose window to commemorate the fact that a swallow built her nest in the half-completed chapel, and 'Great' Sir Thomas forbade the builders to proceed until the nestlings were hatched.

West of the house and near the memorial cross erected in 1873 to the 10th baronet's memory is a fascinating little garden shelter called the 'Bear's Hut' that at one time housed a tame Canadian black bear, later removed to a zoo. It is a rustic hut with a thatched roof, typical of a Victorian garden shelter externally but inside lined with woven matting on walls and ceiling which is decorated with pine cones (see illus 34). The floor is laid in knucklebones of sheep or deer. After the departure of the bear, it became a tea-party

Illus 34 Killerton garden: ceiling of the 'Bear's Hut'

house for children, with faggots always ready in the grate and crockery in the cupboard.

By giving this garden to the Trust, Sir Richard Acland intended that the intelligent care that it has never lacked would be secured. The thirty-five years that have since passed show so well that this intention will be fulfilled.

The House was open to the public for the first time in August–September 1976 for an exhibition of paintings.

Little Haldon, Teignmouth

The B3192 road starts near sea level in the centre of Teignmouth and within 1½ miles has risen to the top of Little Haldon. The summit lies a quarter of a mile off the road at 811ft. To the east of the highway, the Trust were given 43 acres of open heath in 1947, a narrow strip parallel with the road for over three quarters of a mile. There are splendidly extensive views over the whole of the Exe Estuary to the northeast and westwards to Dartmoor.

Lydford Gorge

Turn off the A386 at the Dartmoor Inn 7 miles northeast of Tavistock, following the by-road southwest through the village of

Lydford, and after 2½ miles turn right, across the bridge that crossed the GWR branch line to Launceston and here is the Trust's car park, shop and information centre. The best way to explore the Gorge starts at this point.

The River Lyd rises on Bridestowe Common under Gren Tor three miles to the northeast and originally its course lay to the east of the village, a tributary of the Tavy. From the high ground southwest of the village, a separate stream flowed westwards to join the River Lew at Coryton 3 miles to the west, and so into the Tamar below Lifton. In geological times, this stream cut its way backwards, into and through the watershed which divided it from the Lyd, and so captured the latter, which then poured down the steep route westwards.

The much greater volume of water then gouged out a ravine that is now Lydford Gorge, with rock walls up to 60ft in height. This happened during the glacial period c 450,000 years ago. The potholes in the river bed were formed by swirling boulders.

Lydford was once an important mining town, and for a time during the reign of King Aethelred II, the 'Unready' (978-1016), a mint was established, to strike pennies made of Dartmoor tin. There is a specimen at the Castle Inn nearby. At that time and indeed even now, the parish covered virtually the whole of Dartmoor, an area of 80 square miles. At the southwest end of the village adjoining the church is a massive stone keep, the remains of the prison built in 1195 for the incarceration of prisoners of the Stannary (mining) Court and parliament. It must have been an appalling place for it was described in an Act of Parliament in 1512 as 'one of the most heinous, contagious and detestable places in the realm'; in the time of Henry VIII Richard Strode, the Member for Plympton who fell foul of the Stannary Courts, escaped from the prison. He subsequently took action in Parliament that resulted in recognition of the important principle that all statements made by members in the House of Commons are privileged.

By the seventeenth century, Lydford had declined and the

Illus 35   Lydford Gorge: the Devil's Cauldron

Gorge was inhabited by Roger Rowle 'the local Robin Hood'. He led the Gubbins gang described by Charles Kingsley in *Westward Ho!*, a fearsome and lewd bunch of outlaws!

The ravine began to be an object of interest when the cult of the picturesque started about two centuries ago, and diaries of the period mention 'its awful horrors'! Then the railway came in the summer of 1865, the GWR branch line from Plymouth to Launceston, and the Gorge became famous. It became filled with even more visitors when the LSWR line arrived in Lydford nine years later from the northeast. Although the railways have vanished, alas, the tradition is still kept up by the coach parties.

The walk through the Gorge should be commenced at the south-west end. The path starts at the Trust shop, dropping down and soon passing under the GWR bridge. Then it bifurcates, a notice proclaiming 'LONG AND EASY *or* STEEP AND SHORT'. Either way the visitor is brought down over 100ft to the valley floor, across a foot-bridge to wonder at 'The White Lady', the beautiful single silvery chain of a 100ft waterfall. In the 1860s it was described as the

'Lydford Cascade, one of the prettiest spots imaginable, materially injured by the Tavistock and Launceston Railway. A zigzag walk has been cut and a miller who lives nearby keeps the key to the approach. A certain quantity of water ponded back may, by the magic of sixpence, be made to spring over the fall to which it gives an imposing volume and impetuosity.'

The path now traverses an entrancing glade under Old Cleeve Wood. On either side huge oaks almost roof the Gorge, their trunks covered with lichens, moss and ferns flourish in this aqueous place and the water literally chatters as it pours through clefts from one pothole to the next. Soon the path becomes a narrow ledge cut into the rock face, but the iron handrail gives a complete feeling of safety, and at one point it actually runs through a tunnel. It is probable that the path was first cut in the 1840s since it is recorded in 1850. After one mile, the path reaches the Pixie Glen, running in from the north at right angles, and here it crosses by a footbridge from the northeast side of the river to the southwest side, and starts to climb the rock face. Just before the towering mass of Lydford Bridge looms overhead, there is a narrow side path that leads into the Devil's Cauldron. It ends in a plank whose end is suspended by chains right over an immense pothole, the 'Cauldron' into which the water pours from a narrow cleft. For all the world it is like a place of sacrifice to Poseidon, the water god! It is a very eerie place indeed, and quite sensational (see illus 35).

The main path is then rejoined and climbs steeply up under the bridge to the road again. Note the two arches of the bridge where it has been widened. At this end of the Gorge close to the village, the Trust has purchased further land and a new picnic area and a car park has been constructed. The return to the original starting point can be accomplished along the road, and the visitor will find an excellent inn and tea house at the Manor Hotel adjacent to the car park.

This very splendid place was bought by the Trust between 1943 and 1973, and its area is 115 acres. There were 51,000 visitors in 1976.

Plym Bridge Woods

This is another beautiful wooded river valley where the Trust has acquired 124 acres since 1968, starting at the medieval thirteenth century Plym Bridge in Bickleigh Vale, 4 miles due northeast of the centre of Plymouth, on a narrow road that runs from the A386 at Plymouth Airport to Plympton.

The Trust land runs northwards up the Vale, following the river bed for 2000yd as far as the Riverford viaduct on the old GWR Launceston branch line.

Today it is a peaceful place of trees and water, with bathing and picnicking places beside the river. But it was not so during the first half of the nineteenth century. Halfway up the Trust land are the remains of massive slate workings, Cann Quarry on the east bank of the river, and Rumple Quarry on the west.

Through the woods was laid the Plymouth and Dartmoor

Railway built to transport granite from King Tor near Princetown and opened in September 1823 (track removed 1916). In November 1829 the Cann Canal was opened to take slate from the quarry to the Laira Estuary. The project was sponsored by Earl Morley of Saltram on whose land the canal was cut. This waterway was abandoned as such in 1835, when the Cann Quarry branch of the Plymouth and Dartmoor Railway was laid on its towpath and opened in 1834 (track also removed 1916). The quarries closed in 1855, but there was further activity when the GWR constructed its line from Plymouth to Tavistock through the woods in 1858-9.

The path through the woods starts at a gate 150yd northeast of Plym bridge and, after a distance of half a mile, the massive 1907 blue-brick GWR Cann viaduct is reached. Alongside it on each side of the river are to be seen the massive stone foundation piers of Brunel's 1858 timber viaduct that carried the line over the Plym. Just under the viaduct, the path passes the 'wheel pit' of the quarry. It is easy to walk along the top of the stone walls of this structure, 6oft long, 6ft wide and about 25ft in depth. It would have housed the very large 5oft waterwheel mentioned in *The Handbook for Travellers*: 'the stone is drawn from the quarry and the drainage effected by water-machinery, and just beyond it is the Weir-head in the shape of a crescent.' This weir was built to impound water for the canal, which flowed through a tunnel under the viaduct before emerging into the north end of the canal. South of the Cann viaduct are the ruins of several quarry workers' cottages and the canal, which can still be seen, was used until recently as a leat to take water from the Weir to Marsh Mills china clay dry.

There is an excellent nature walk in these woods fully described in the Country Walks Booklet, with a wealth of detail about the trees and flora generally, also the ravens' nests in Cann Quarry, (the fishing is let to the Plymouth and District Freshwater Angling Association). It is as well to note that although the Trust's ownership includes nearly all the track of the old GWR line from Plym Bridge northwestwards for $1\frac{1}{2}$ miles almost to Riverford Viaduct, it does *not* include a length of 200yd centred on Cann Viaduct, neither does it include the leat from its northern end to Plym Bridge.

Rockbeare Hill

2½ miles west-south-west of the village of Ottery St Mary on the B3180 road is the first site in Devon given to the Trust in 1904, 22 acres of Scots pine and heath on a hill top. It is also called Prickly Pear Blossoms Park and has extensive views over East Devon towards Exeter. When it was given to the Trust by Mr W. H. B. Nation (appropriate name) he imposed a condition that the growth of the Prickly Pear should be fostered.

The main part of the land has in recent years been opened to encourage its use, the western sector being mainly woodland, and the eastern an open space, justifying its designation on a number of maps as 'recreation ground'. It is an important site because it restricts further encroachment by the quarry company who are operating the gravel pits to the north.

Withleigh

Three miles southwest of the centre of Tiverton and on the south-east side of the A373 Tiverton–South Molton road are 139 acres of water meadows flanked by deciduous woodland in a delightful hidden valley of the Little Dart, 3 miles below its source. It is called Buzzards at the wish of the donor because of the activity of these birds over the property.

In 1967 82 acres of coppice and meadow was given: this is Buzzards. Sir John Heathcoat-Amory of Knightshayes added 27 acres of Huntland Wood on the east bank of the river in 1970 and the Trust purchased a further 30 acres of steep pasture on the northeast bank at Nethercleave in 1971.

Access is off the A373 road keeping straight on in Withleigh at the T sign until the Trust's car park is reached after half a mile. There are two long bridle-paths and a footpath running through the property which is 1½ miles from end to end. It is a sequestered place, specially quiet and beautiful, ideal for Trust members who seek solitude and exercise for themselves and their dogs.

8 Inland Landscape of Cornwall

Ardevora

The Truro river joins up with the River Fal just below the great house Tregothnan and its deer park on the east bank of the Truro river 3 miles southeast of Truro. The Fal rises away up to the northeast of Treviscoe, and before it silted up due to mineral workings, ships could navigate inland to Tregony. The existence of a large limekiln at Ruan quay, over 3 miles up from the confluence, is proof of seaborne trade.

The Trust own 54 acres of foreshore and saltings on the south bank of the Fal between Ruanlanihorne and Tregothnan, and they are all leased to the Cornwall Naturalists' Trust as a Nature Reserve. They comprise typical muddy foreshore with saltmarsh vegetation and a feeding ground for birds.

The more easterly of the two separate areas starts on the south bank opposite Ruan, runs west and then southwest into and up to the limit of Tuckingmill Creek, half a mile inland. This is due west of Trelonk, and the area is 22 acres, acquired in 1966.

The second area starts on the south shore immediately adjoining Ardevora Farm and runs for one mile westwards, into and up to the inner limits of the two creeks west of that farm.

Cadson Bury

The most advantageous way to see Cadson Bury is to take the lane that leads northwest from St Mellion via Amy Tree to Newbridge. The last half a mile runs down the steep hill leading into the valley, and from the west side of this lane an excellent view of the site is obtained, particularly in morning sunlight.

It is a slightly mysterious place, an imposing and isolated hill towering up on the west side of the valley of the River Lynher with a narrow lane running north–south along its eastern base. It is in the parish of St Ive (pronounced 'Eve') and can be missed on that account because it is so often associated with Callington, 2 miles to the northeast.

It is a scheduled Ancient Monument, still not yet excavated but probably an early Iron Age hill fortress c fifth–third centuries BC, commanding the river valley to the south. There is a car park on the river bank, and a signposted path to the 425ft summit from the southern end of the hill. Its 84 acres were acquired in 1970.

Chapel Carn Brea

The road traversed by tens of thousands of tourists every year to unlovely Land's End passes under the 657ft summit of Chapel Carn Brea lying inland 1½ miles from the Atlantic coast. It is described 'Carn Brea' on the 1in Ordnance Survey map, the second word being pronounced 'Bray'.

At one time it was crowned with a great stone cairn and, in medieval times, surmounted by a hermitage chapel dedicated to St Michael where the custodian kept a beacon for the guidance of fishermen, in effect a pharos.

The Handbook for Travellers describes the site eloquently

'it should be climbed for the sake of the prospect which from the small girth of this part of the peninsula includes a wonderful expanse of water. Three seas roll in sight, and the eye ranging around 28 points of compass reposes during the interval on their azure surface.'

This view is claimed as the widest sea view in the British Isles.

The cairn was terribly mauled by military occupation during

World War II, but a small stone 'cist' (slab coffin) can be seen on the south side. The Ordnance Survey map shows two tumuli.

This hill of 53 acres was acquired in 1971, and access on foot is from the lane skirting the northeast of the hill from Crows-an-Wra on the A30 to Land's End Airport.

Cotehele Walk

The Country Walks booklet gives a detailed walk of 1½ miles around the Cotehele estate to explore the riverside and woods that form the setting of this house, for the detailed description of which see Chapter 6.

The walk starts at the car park on Cotehele Quay, runs east up the valley, passing Morden Mill on the opposite side of the valley, turning northeast to reach the mansion, thence down to the Tamar cliff, past the 'Chapel on the Cliff' (see page 86) and finally southwards to reach the car park.

Erth Barton and Island

One of the least spoiled areas in southeast Cornwall is the beautiful river valley from St Germans Quay to Antony Park on the south shore, called the St Germans or Lynher River. From the northwest end of Erth Island for a mile southeast as far as the western shore of the bay west of Black Rock, 198 acres of saltings and saltmarsh were given to the Trust in 1962 by the Duchy of Cornwall and Sir John Carew-Pole. They lie 1½ miles southeast of St Germans.

Glendurgan Garden

Glendurgan is a steep-sided little valley running southwards to the north shore of the Helford River with access from the road from Mawnan Smith to Helford Passage. It is in a defined Area of Outstanding Natural Beauty.

The 40 acres owned by the Trust here comprise Glendurgan House and its gardens together with the beach and eight cottages.

Many years ago when the river was famous for fish and lobster, these cottages were lived in by fishermen and their families. They owned donkeys and there were times when, after a good haul, as many as 23 donkeys, tied head to tail, panniers on each side, would be led by the fishermen's wives into Falmouth Market.

The garden here will for ever be associated with the Quaker family of Fox, the first recorded member of that family to live in Cornwall being Francis (from Wiltshire) who married Dorothy Kekewich and settled at Catchfrench 3 miles from St Germans c 1645. Later the family moved to Fowey and then in 1759 to Falmouth where ever since they have been associated with port affairs as G. C. Fox and Company, Consuls, Ship Agents and Merchants. During the past 218 years generations of Foxs have carried on the business and have represented thirty-five countries in a consular capacity. They are proud to possess in their office Deeds of Appointment signed by George Washington (30 May 1794) and Abraham Lincoln (11 March 1863). In the Falmouth Tercentenary Book (1662–1962) one reads 'one of their notable country houses is Glendurgan set in a lovely garden' (see illus 11).

The garden was originally planted in the 1820s–30s by Alfred Fox, and he built a thatched cottage which was soon burnt down. Shortly afterwards, he erected the present house (c 1830) where the family still live. Alfred's son George Henry came into possession in 1851; he was a keen botanist and naturalist. His son Cuthbert became the owner in 1936, and he and his son Philip gave the property to the Trust in 1962.

The garden falls away invitingly down the 'glen'. Alfred planted the laurel maze in 1833, and he must have been responsible for planting many of the fine trees and serpentine paths laid out in the romantic manner. Glendurgan is warm and sheltered, tender exotic plants thrive, providing infinite variety in shape and colour throughout the year. Noted specimens include two immense tulip trees, a weeping swamp cypress, a weeping Mexican cypress, and a Japanese loquat. In spring the garden is scattered with Lent lilies, primroses and later bluebells, and glows with magnolias, cherries, camellias and rhododendrons. Later the hydrangeas and eucryphias take over. To the northwest of the house, there is a wall garden with Irish yews and juniper and *Itea ilicifolia* hung with green catkins in summer.

Lanhydrock Walk

The Country Walks booklet gives a detailed walk of 2 miles around the park of Lanhydrock, starting at the house, running east to Newton Lodge, thence south to the northwest bank of the Fowey River, with the main Plymouth–Penzance railway constructed 1852–5, opened 1859, opposite, and finally northwest to finish at the house, for tea in the restaurant. This is a delightful excursion on a warm spring or summer afternoon, designed to show many different types of trees, wild flowers and birds. The description in the booklet is an essential pre-requisite.

Lerryn Creek

The water of Lerryn Creek joins the main Fowey river $2\frac{1}{2}$ miles north of Fowey. The creek runs for $2\frac{1}{2}$ miles up to its head at the old harbour of Lerryn, a place to which small schooners and barges formerly came with coal, and lime to be burnt in the kilns, and to collect produce from the local mill. It is a quiet and lovely place.

Looking across the creek, in a pastoral landscape of woods and fields, is Ethy House and its wooded park. The mansion is a plain late-Georgian brick building, the centre flanked with giant pilasters. There is a walled garden with palms.

Ethy, not open to the public, was given to the Trust as an endowment for St Michael's Mount and is not inalienable. The estate covers 377 acres, and there is a splendid creekside walk from Lerryn to Ethy Wood, thence up the valley to St Winnow Mill.

Rough Tor

Bodmin Moor is the last great wilderness in the southwest, and is rightly described as an Area of Outstanding Natural Beauty. It fully meets the requirements of landscape of National Park quality despite its china clay workings and inevitable power cables. In the name of tourism, it is constantly under threat.

Its two highest points, indeed the highest 'mountains' in Cornwall, are Brown Willy at 1377ft and Rough Tor at 1311ft, lying 3–4 miles due southeast of Camelford.

The air here is vigorous, smelling of heather and ling, and there are the glimpses of the two seas, the Channel 19 miles to the southeast, and the Atlantic coast of Cornwall only 7 miles to the northwest. The view is 'all the greater for what it suggests rather than reveals' (E. F. Bozman 1940).

The splendid summit of Rough Tor from about the 950ft contour upwards, together with 174 acres of moorland in all, was given to the Trust in 1951 by Sir Richard Onslow, with the World War II memorial to the men of the 43rd Wessex Division. The 1in Ordnance Survey map shows 'Tumulus', 'Logan Rock' and 'Hut Circles' here, and indeed it is a Bronze Age settlement site with enclosed fields, some with lynchets. Ancient man came to the moor about five thousand years ago, and a thousand years later c 2000 BC came the Beaker folk who probably gave the lead in exporting Cornish tin and Irish copper and gold.

Access by car to Rough Tor is via the Jubilee Drive that runs due southeast from the A39 at Camelford for 2 miles to Rough Tor farm. From here it is another 1½ miles on foot to the summit.

Trelissick Garden

At Turnaware Point, the River Fal opens out into the northern end of the Carrick Roads, a magnificent sheet of deep water north of Falmouth, 4 miles long and a mile wide. To the north of the Point lies the park of Trelissick with its great neo-Greek house. The prospect of this park seen from the deck of a boat sailing up the Roads is quite superb. (See illus 36.)

Little is known of any early history of Trelissick, but a mansion

(*overleaf*) *Illus 36* The park of Trelissick near Truro looking south over the Carrick Roads

house was built about 1750 by John Lawrence, a captain in the Cornwall militia during the Seven Years' War in Europe (1756–63). He was still remembered in the 1830s for his convivial habits and 'wild eccentricities' (in an age of eccentrics!); a pleasant memory of a man who had chosen such a superb site to build his house. The architect for the building was Edmund Davy and an engraving of 1820 shows a villa with a columned verandah and wings.

Lawrence died c 1790, and at the turn of the century the property was purchased by Ralph Allen Daniell, then probably the richest man in Cornwall. His father was Thomas Daniell whose elegant Mansion House, completed in 1762, still exists in Truro. He started his career as clerk to Sir William Lemon, a leading figure in Cornish mining. His wealth passed on his death to his son, who married Elizabeth Elliott, a niece of the Cornishman, Ralph Allen, who made a fortune of half a million pounds when postmaster at Bath in the eighteenth century. Ralph Allen Daniell was carried along on the floodtide of Cornish mining prosperity, and from Wheal Towan at Porthtowan, not far from Wheal Coates (see page 159), he is said to have received £150,000 in a few years. This mine was worked extensively for copper between 1790 and 1824, and is recorded as producing £250,000 profit before 1843. He was member of parliament for West Looe and died in 1823, to be succeeded by his son Thomas, who employed Peter Robinson, architect (1776–1858), to reconstruct Trelissick in 1825. Robinson was a pupil of Henry Holland and he incorporated Davy's 1750 house in the rebuilt mansion, which has a six-column giant Ionic portico, copying that of the Erechtheion at Athens.

Thomas Daniell lived in great splendour, laying out miles of rides and carriage roads through the beautiful woods along the west bank of the Fal but, large though his income was and with the new mansion only just complete, he sold the whole property in 1832 and left the country.

Trelissick was then purchased by the Earl of Falmouth, who in turn sold it to John Davies Gilbert in 1844 and it remained in that family until 1913. During this period, a second storey was added to the wings. The Gilbert executors let the property to a governor of the Bank of England, Leonard Cunliffe, in 1913; he purchased it in 1928 leaving it on his death in 1937 to his step-daughter Mrs Ida Copeland. She gave the House with 376 acres of parkland and woods and Turnaware Point on the east bank of the river to the Trust in 1955.

Mrs Copeland's husband, Ronald, was managing director of the Spode china factory between 1913–55 (many 'Spode' flowers were grown here), and it is to them both that the present Trelissick garden is largely due. When they started it, it was largely a shrubbery of mauve *Rhododendron ponticum*, laurel and other shrubs. They planted a great new range of rhododendrons and azaleas, as well as choice trees and shrubs. Trelissick is given its character by spacious lawns, winding walks which lead under great beeches and holm oaks, with magnolias, eucalyptus, and maples. Across a footbridge over the road to King Harry Ferry, a path leads to a recently reclaimed area called Carcadden. This area contains big cedars, cypresses and geans, and a collection of over 130 species of hydrangea. While many Cornish gardens fade into summer greenery, Trelissick is colourful until the fall.

There is a car park at the entrance on the B3289 road 5 miles south of Truro and a garden shop. The house is not open.

Trencrom

This magnificent hilltop of 64 acres was presented to the Trust in 1946 by Colonel Gifford Tyringham of Trevethoe, one mile to the northeast, a descendant of William Praed who promoted the Grand Junction Canal from London to Birmingham in 1790. It was given as a war memorial in memory of the men and women of Cornwall who died in two World Wars. It is reached by the turning off the A3074 at Trevethoe Lodge, Lelant, and taking the road west to Lelant Downs. Here there are two lanes that give access to the base of the hill, one runs west-north-west to Trencrom Farm with two entrances to the site off it. The other runs due west to the Trust's car park and shop.

The name for this 'Camp', (it is so marked on the 1in Ordnance

Survey map) is taken from the farm adjoining it to the northwest: 'Trencrom', more correctly *Tre'n-crobben*, in Cornish, 'the farm of the crooked hill'. It is a well preserved Iron Age B hill- fort, stone walled and enclosing hut circles. From its summit over 500ft above sea level, there is a fine prospect of Cornish countryside, northeast to St Agnes Beacon and southeast to the Lizard. It forms a natural outpost for the Penwith peninsula, and the hilltop consists of two large outcrops of granite with a saddle of one acre of turf between them. It is possible to trace the line of a single unditched rampart which utilised rock outcrops for much of its course. Huge granite boulders have been pushed into shape and built up behind with smaller stones, turf and gravel. Inside the fortress, traces of circular huts of the early Iron Age are visible, rather like rough saucers, outlined by walls of granite blocks. Unexcavated, Trencrom goes back to the second century BC on the strength of surface finds of stray pottery; two polished greenstone axes of Neolithic type were found some years ago on the lower slopes. It may well be that during the troubled times of the Saxon advance into Cornwall in the eighth–ninth centuries, the Cornish took refuge in this ancient stronghold. This is suggested by shards of 'grassmarked' pottery peculiar to Cornwall in the Dark Ages, that have been found here. The Ceremony of the Gorsedd of the Bards of Cornwall, founded in 1928, was held on Trencrom in 1953.

A quarter of a mile to the northeast of the site on the side of the main coach road to St Ives is a curious and very large granite boulder called the Bowl Rock. This was given to the Trust in 1962.

Trengwainton Garden

The Cornish name Trengwainton is derived from *Tre-an-gwaynten* 'the farm of the spring', and the mansion and garden of that name lie 1½ miles northwest of the centre of Penzance, set at the foot of the granite hills that lie behind Penzance. The name is apt for what has become a garden rich in tender plants.

The name is recorded in the thirteenth century and there has been a dwelling on the site for at least four hundred years. There is also a stone in the wall of the enclosed garden with the date 1692–3 that marks the acquisition of the property by the Arundell family who built Trerice (see page 101).

In 1814, Trengwainton was purchased by Rose Price, the son of a wealthy Jamaican sugar planter. He was created a baronet the following year. He planted trees on a considerable scale, beech, ash and sycamore in the main, and constructed a series of walled gardens with raised terraced beds and three ponds, one being a duck decoy. There was also an ice house.

Sir Rose Price died in 1834 the year after Samuel Wilberforce's Emancipation Act which freed the slaves, including those at Worthy Park, Jamaica, from which his income derived, and in 1836 Trengwainton was sold by his heir to mortgagees. It is a curious quirk of history that Wilberforce's partner Thomas Clarkson owned the special lectern chair now in the Library at Trerice (see page 106).

In 1867, the property was bought by Thomas Simon Bolitho, a Cornish banker particularly involved in tin smelting and his son Thomas Robins Bolitho enlarged the Regency house in 1897 and built a wide carriage drive to the east of the wood leading to the still extant Georgian lodge c 1820.

Trengwainton passed to his nephew Lt-Col Edward Bolitho in 1925, a great Cornishman, Chairman of the County Council 1941–52, Lord-Lieutenant of Cornwall in 1936 and knighted in 1953. He died in 1969.

Very little gardening had been done before 1925 but 'the Colonel', as he was always known, at once took it up actively. Three great Cornish gardeners, J. C. Williams of Caerhayes Castle, P. D. Williams of Lanarth and Canon A. T. Boscawen of Ludgvan, took a very close interest in the new venture, and provided Trengwainton Garden with many gifts of rhododendrons and other shrubs from New Zealand, Australia, Chile and the Himalayas.

In 1926, George Johnstone of Trewithen, then owner of a most beautiful garden between Truro and St Austell, and Major Lawrence Johnston of Hidcote Manor near Chipping Campden – another Trust garden since 1948 – offered Colonel Bolitho a share in F. Kingdom Ward's 1927–8 expedition to northeast Assam and the Mishmi Hills in Upper Burma. Another subscriber to this expedition was Sir Francis Acland of Killerton.

It is from seed obtained from this overseas trip that the rhododendron collection of Trengwainton was largely founded, and it was due to the skill of the head gardener, A. Creek, that these very tender seedlings were raised so successfully. *R. macabeanum*, *R. elliottii*, *R. Taggianum*, and *R. concateanus* were flowered here for the first time in the British Isles. Most of them were planted in the shelter of Rose Price's plantations, and several of his walled gardens were used to establish many other tender plants.

After thirty years' service Creek was succeeded in 1934 by G. W. Thomas. G. Hulbert (1948–59) was in charge when the stream garden was planted with masses of primulas and other moisture-loving plants. P. Horder the present head gardener came to Trengwainton in 1970 after completing his course at Wisley.

In 1961, Sir Edward received the coveted Victorian Medal of Honour for Horticulture, and that same year he vested the property in the Trust, together with the park and woodland, in all 98 acres. From then on, this splendid and beautiful garden (see illus 37) on which so much care and love has been expended during the last fifty years has been open to the public. Sir Edward died in 1969, and the house is now occupied by his son Major Simon Bolitho. It is not open. Access is from the road joining Heamoor with the A3071 road at Tremethick Cross.

Illus 37   The sub-tropical garden at Trengwainton near Penzance

9 Miscellaneous Buildings

DEVON

Boringdon Gate Piers

In 1712, George Parker of North Molton and Boringdon, ancestor of the Earls of Morley, purchased Saltram (qv). His son, John Parker, married the Lady Catherine Poulett, daughter of Earl Poulett, Secretary of State to Queen Anne. Thirty years later, John and his wife commenced rebuilding Saltram and transferred the family residence from Boringdon, north of Plympton, 2 miles south-west to the new site overlooking the Laira Estuary. Boringdon House was described in 1862 as 'anciently the residence of the Parkers, built about 1350 but with few remains'. It is still marked on Ordnance Survey maps with gothic letters.

Boringdon originally had four pairs of very good granite gate piers. One pair is now at the Stag Lodge entrance to Saltram: a second is at Fardell 4½ miles due east near Cornwood, originally the home of Sir Walter Raleigh's family (see Compton Castle p 69), the third pair is on its original site, whilst the fourth remains on the east side of the narrow lane that leads from Plympton to Plym Bridge, and approximately half a mile southeast of the bridge. They afforded the western access to Boringdon Deer Park, and were given to the Trust in 1961 by the 5th Earl of Morley.

Hartland, East Titchberry Cottage

This is a Trust holiday cottage, lying close to the picturesque group of thatched farm buildings at East Titchberry and five minutes on foot from Shipload Bay and the sea. There are lovely walks along the cliffs with a view to Lundy Island and the South Wales coast (see page 23). It sleeps five.

(See details in the booklet 'Cornish Holiday Cottages.')

Loughwood Meeting House

This fascinating mid-seventeenth century Baptist chapel is a little difficult to locate but it is marked by a tiny cross on the 1in Ordnance Survey map (sheet 177) next to the words 'Loughwood Farm', $2\frac{3}{4}$ miles west-north-west of Axminster. It is in the parish of Dalwood, and a lane leads off obliquely from the A35. There is a tiny sign in the hedge.

The first reference to it was in 1653 when the Baptist congregation at Kilmington, $1\frac{1}{2}$ miles southeast, sought refuge from persecution 'in a remote place'. It is one of the earliest Baptist chapels in England; at that time Dalwood was actually in Dorset.

The chapel is built in local grey stone rubble with the roof covered in thatch. Inside, the fittings are early eighteenth century and are virtually intact. The walls are white, the windows clear glazed, some with early nineteenth century Gothick glazing bars, the pews are of unvarnished pine, there is a high set pulpit and gallery, underneath which there are two retiring rooms, one for each sex, each with a tiny fireplace. Here the congregation spent their time between morning and evening service, in talk and instruction of their children. Beneath the pulpit is the baptismal tank.

The adjoining stone and cob building, with a clay pantiled roof, was the stable where the minister parked his horse, and around the site are the graves of former members of this quiet rural church, which was in active use until 1833.

The building was renovated in 1871 when the roof was sheeted with corrugated iron, but by 1960 the fabric had become so decayed that all services were stopped. An appeal for funds was then launched and some monies came in, but in 1969 it was transferred by the Devon and Cornwall Baptist Corporation Ltd to the Trust. A complete restoration was then carried out with the funds afore-mentioned together with a grant from the Historic Buildings Council and another from the Axminster RDC. Both church and burial ground are still available for religious use.

The name of this chapel is pronounced 'Luffwood'.

Moretonhampstead Almshouses

The Handbook for Travellers remarked in 1865, 'In Moreton-hampstead, the houses are mean and thatched and, with the exception of the poor-house, which has an arched arcade of the 17th century, there is nothing worth notice'.

For 'poor house', read Almshouses, given to the Trust in 1952 by the Moretonhampstead Almshouse Charity. The building is on the north side of the B3212 road on the eastern edge of the town, and is a stone structure in squared and coursed granite, with a slate roof. The arcade is wholly delightful, five arched openings, with columns, and a central opening giving access to a covered corridor, reminiscent of the Rows at Chester on a smaller scale. It was erected in 1637, and is not open.

Parke, Bovey Tracey

Running west out of the town, the B3344 road leads to the entrance gate of the mansion and park of Parke. It is bounded on the east by the track of the former GWR branch line from Newton Abbot that ran for 12½ miles up the Bovey Valley to Moretonhampstead between 1866 and 1959, where 'a vehicle will meet you and take you to the GWR Manor House Hotel with all creature comforts assured'. (GWR advertisement.)

The estate of Parke was at one time Crown land and in 1571 was leased to a Thomas Southcot. The house on it was of fourteenth century date and castellated. In 1825, the property was conveyed to William Hole of Stickwick and he immediately demolished the medieval house (no conservationists to thwart him!). The new house which, with its 205 acres of parkland, passed to the Trust in

1976, was built between 1827 and 1828, and was given by Major M. A. Hole, a descendant of William Hole. The main southeast front presents an austere late-Georgian house in yellow stucco, with a central portico on two pairs of plain Greek Doric columns. In front is an elliptical lawn and carriage sweep, with a fine prospect over the park, and a panoramic view to the northeast over the valley and hills beyond. The Dartmoor National Park boundary is close by. Behind the house is a little wooded knoll with a serpentine walk leading up into the woods. There is a curious nail-studded back door to the house that may have survived from its medieval predecessor. Parke is not yet open to the public. Separated from Parke on the northeast side of the valley are 34 acres of woodland at Bearacleave, three-quarters of a mile due north of the town, rising steeply to over 600ft.

Shute Barton

This historic property is situated south of the A35 on the B3161 road 2 miles north of Colyton, and 3 miles west-south-west of Axminster. It was acquired from Sir John Carew-Pole of Antony (qv) in 1959, and repaired with money found by him and from a bequest. The land then conveyed, 5 acres, has since been increased to $15\frac{1}{2}$ acres.

Shute is one of the more important surviving non-castellated dwelling houses of the Middle Ages. Sir William Bonville, Sheriff of Devon in 1390, began it c 1380, building what is now the southeast wing. It was enlarged by the Greys, Marquises of Dorset, when they acquired it by marriage in 1476. They built the northeast wing. Henry Grey, who was created Duke of Suffolk and beheaded in 1554 for rebellion against Queen Mary, was the father of Lady Jane Grey who also lost her head by execution on 12 February of the same year.

A few years later, Shute was acquired by Sir William (de la) Pole, and he made further additions to the house, and built the gatehouse c 1570. This structure with flat-arched windows and mullions of the late Elizabethan period was the entrance to a typical late Tudor forecourt. The initials WP and the motto, *Pollet virtus*, of the Pole family, appear in the heraldic work. The gazebos flanking the house were built about a century ago, replacing thatched *cottages ornées* in the late Georgian taste.

Where the drive now runs stood the 'Great House' of the Tudor period which was demolished in 1785 when Shute House was built half a mile away (completed in 1787).

The façade of the late fourteenth and late fifteenth centuries is interesting in that it is of flint with ashlar dressings, a mode of construction used so often in chalk districts. The nineteenth century school at nearby Colyton is faced with large pieces of squared blue flint. At the junction of the fourteenth and fifteenth century work, there is an angled turret with a newel staircase.

The exterior of this property can be viewed in daylight at any time. Access to the interior is by appointment only from the Trust's tenant, Patrick Rice. The rooms of chief interest are the kitchen on the ground floor with an enormous fireplace separated from an adjoining room by a studded partition of medieval date. Above the kitchen is the hall with trussed roof and carved wind-braces. To the north of the hall is a room that was possibly the solar, but was panelled c 1650.

A full architectural history of Shute will be found in two issues of *Country Life*, 2 and 9 February 1957.

Tiverton, Old Blundells School

Peter Blundell, a rich clothier, founded this well-known school in 1604, at the beginning of the reign of King James I. It prospered and in 1882 a new school was built and the original early seventeenth century building was sold. It had housed two classrooms, the higher and lower schools, and the dining hall, and reputedly contained timbers from wrecked Armada ships.

In the 1880s, the building was converted into dwelling houses, but was bought in 1940 by the Old Blundellian Club and presented to the school governors in 1945. As seen from the junction of Gold Street, Blundell's Road and Station Road, this Stuart building shows a long structure in eleven bays, faced in squared warm golden sandstone with a slated roof. Two of the bays have porches with semi-circular arches and a niche, whilst the southeast porch has a cupola, with a bell and clock and a weather-vane bearing the initials PB. On the wall the names of past scholars are to be found carved in the stonework.

The building is not open to visitors, but there is a pleasant forecourt of grass lawn bordered with pollarded limes. There is also an attractive gateway between two porters' lodges with an arch formed by the chimney flues from these lodges. On the 350th anniversary of the foundation in 1954, these houses with 3 acres of ground were given to the Trust by the Governors with aid from the Pilgrim Trust and the Goldsmiths' Company. The forecourt only is open.

Widecombe-in-the-Moor Church House

This village in the heart of Dartmoor lies on the East Webburn River, a tributary of the Dart, and is 4 miles north of New Bridge and Holne Woods (see page 110). A lane runs up the valley from the bridge to the village.

It has been immortalised in the folk-song 'Widecombe Fair', and is best known for its splendid fifteenth century church and 120ft high tower. W. G. Hoskins writes of the place 'best seen in winter as the village has been terribly commercialised. The church remains unspoilt by all this vulgarity. Church House near by, built about 1500, is one of the best of its kind in Devon'.

Church House, part-cottage, part-village hall, was purchased by the Trust in 1933 from local funds.

CORNWALL

Holiday Cottages

The work of the Trust has many facets, and one of them is the holiday cottages. A number of its properties include cottages, often fallen into disuse as the pattern of local life has changed, among them are fishermen's dwellings, those occupied by gamekeepers or forestry workers, even a water tower, as well as net lofts, village schools, a mine engine house, and so on. Often picturesque, they are good examples of the local architectural vernacular and have been made into really comfortable furnished cottages. The use of redundant buildings in this perfectly laudable fashion helps the Trust's finances, badly needed to meet the ever-increasing cost of upkeep, and at the same time enables people to enjoy a holiday in idyllic surroundings. Full information about renting is contained in the Cottages Booklet, together with details of caretakers, and a description of the cottages is given below.

Boscastle, 6 miles from Camelford

1 Harbour View
A house at the head of the harbour just above the Manor Bridge, looking down to the quays. It sleeps six.

Cotehele

2 Danescombe Cottage
This lies about half a mile up a wooded valley northwest of Danescombe Quay and Hotel. The 6in Ordnance Survey map indicates this site as the disused Cotehele Consols Copper and Arsenic Mine, one of a group of such mines under the general title of Calstock Mines, which was working about 1856. The cottage was the mine manager's house. There is access for a car and it sleeps four.

3 Enquire Cottage

This was the original building that housed the small beam engine at this mine. It sleeps three, and adjoins Danescombe Cottage.

4 Morden Mill

Morden Mill lies half a mile west of Cotehele Quay and is on a public road. It has been the manor mill of the Cotehele estate since early medieval times. Part of it has been converted as a holiday cottage and sleeps four. For details of the mill itself see Chapter 10 p 160.

5 Old Stan's Cottage: Cotehele Quay

This cottage takes its name from a former occupier Stanley Langford, a fisherman. It faces across the quay and over the Tamar looking into Devonshire. It sleeps five.

Durgan, Helford River

6 Wood Cottage

This is a small thatched timber cottage formerly an apple store. It is near Glendurgan Garden and sleeps four.

7 Old School House

This is situated immediately above the beach at Durgan at the foot of the valley below the garden. It sleeps four.

Helford

8 Penarvon Bungalow

Just over a mile southwest of Durgan on the southern shore of the Helford River is Penarvon Bungalow, a small timber cottage set on a bluff above Penarvon Cove. Helford village is only a few hundred yards away. The bungalow has a fine view over the mouth of the river. It sleeps four.

Land's End

9 Trevescan Farm House

The Cornish name is possibly *Tref-heskyn* 'a farm by a marsh', and the hamlet lies on the B3315 road three-quarters of a mile due east of Land's End Hotel and half a mile south of Sennen Churchtown. The house is a little granite cottage sleeping five. The walk from here along the cliffs to Porthgwarra is perhaps the finest in Cornwall.

Lanteglos-by-Fowey and Lansallos

10 Pont Creek Cottage, Lanteglos

A stream rises at Lanreath and runs into Fowey Harbour at Pont Pill, 5 miles to the southwest. A mile upstream from the harbour is Pont, the bridgehead, where there is a small cottage that sleeps four, one of a group of buildings at the Creek head, (see also p 53).

11 Lansallos Barton

Lansallos, 2 miles east of Pont, is a tiny Cornish 'churchtown' ie that part of the parish centred round the church and spelt in Cornish *treveglos*. Lansallos is small and still unspoiled. The Barton has been divided into two flats, the West House sleeps five, and the East House four.

12 Frogmore Farm House

This lies on the coast and is between Lansallos and Polruan, marked on the 1in Ordnance Survey map, and has been divided into two flats. Both sleep four.

13 Triggabrowne

This is a lovely vernacular Cornish building, its walls hung with silver grey slates, and is on the coast road half a mile west of Frogmore. The house sleeps four; there is a separate flat to sleep three.

14 Triggabrowne Cottage

Within a short distance of the last is this cottage that sleeps four.

Port Gaverne

15 This small cove, immediately adjoining Port Isaac to the east, was in constant use until c 1895 for the export of slate from Delabole. Horsedrawn carts came down from the quarry $5\frac{1}{2}$ miles away to load into the holds of 6oft smacks and schooners on the beach, although there was also a quay, still to be seen. This cottage is in the middle of a huddle of fishermen's buildings 100yd from the beach. It sleeps seven, and an additional bedroom is available.

Portquin

At one time this was a small but active fishing cove where huge quantities of pilchards were landed, packed into hogsheads, salted and sent to Italy and other countries. The huge Cornish pilchard industry ended early this century. The Trust now owns the south side of the tiny harbour and the cottages let for holidays.

16 Carolina Cellar
Formerly a fishermen's net loft, situated at the head of the harbour, and sleeps four.

17 Quin Cottage
It lies just behind the beach and sleeps six. It is a typical north Cornish cottage and has been beautifully restored (see illus 38).

18 Lacombe
A pretty little cottage above Carolina Cellar sleeping four.

19 Doyden House
This was built by a governor of Pentonville Prison about 1870, and has a later tower. It has been divided into five flats.
   Kellan (ground floor) to sleep two; Carnweather (ground floor) to sleep four; Trevan (ground floor) to sleep five; The Rumps (first floor) to sleep two; The Mouls (first floor) to sleep four.

Illus 38   Quin Cottage, Port Quin, North Cornwall: one of thirty-one holiday
cottages owned by the Trust in Cornwall

20 Doyden Castle

This is a picturesque 'folly' on the cliff edge north of Doyden
House. It was built about 1830 by Samuel Symons of Gonvena, a
handsome 1780 house near Wadebridge. Symons used to ride out
from Gonvena to dice and drink as the ample wine bins in the
'Castle' cellar bear witness. It is a rectangular building with bays,
the walls being constructed of brown sandstone squared and
coursed. The windows on the first floor are Gothick; those on the
ground floor are flat arched with labels, all in granite. The roof is
battlemented with corner finials. It will be recognised by television
addicts as Dr Dwight Enys' house in the series *Poldark*. It sleeps
three and is not suitable for children as it is on the cliff edge. There
are quite spectacular views.

St Anthony-in-Roseland

St Anthony Head forms the eastern entrance to Falmouth Harbour,
and lies at the southern end of the Roseland Peninsula (see page 49).
A coast artillery battery was established on the top of the cliffs
about eighty years ago and the Trust purchased it from the War
Department in 1959, then cleared the ugly World War II huts.

21 St Anthony Fort

The former officers' mess, commanding officer's quarters, and the blacksmith's shop, all of Edward VII's period, and built of stone, have been converted into four holiday cottages.

The Lieutenant's Quarter to sleep three; The Major's Quarter to sleep six; The Captain's Quarter to sleep four; The Smithy Cottage to sleep four.

22 Lowlands Cottage

This cottage, which sleeps four, is well situated on the east bank of the Porthcuel River opposite St Mawes. It can *only* be reached by boat or on foot from Place Manor, St Anthony, where cars can be parked. It is not suitable for the elderly or for very young children.

23 Old School House, Bohortha

The hamlet of Bohortha lies 1 mile northeast of the old battery and on the road that leads to it from Gerrans. The Old School House, a dame school, is a charming Gothick building c 1830. It ceased to be used as a school about 1920, and has been converted into a cottage to sleep two.

24 Porth Farm Cottage

Porth Farm is half a mile northeast of Bohortha and the cottage, which is a few minutes' walk from Towan Beach, sleeps six.

25 Penhaligon's Cottage

A pretty little thatched cottage at Porth that sleeps four.

Trelissick

26 Bosanko's Cottage

A one-time gamekeeper's cottage on the edge of a wood immediately above King Harry Ferry, and adjoining the ferrymen's cottages. It sleeps four.

Illus 39 The splendid water tower at Trelissick c 1860. Now available for rent as a holiday cottage

27 The Water Tower

Before the Trelissick estate and its mansion had its own reservoir, water was provided from a very tall water tower, built about 1860. It is a fascinating local stone building, circular with a rounded bay, topped with a dunce-cap slated roof with small gabled dormers and the windows are pointed Gothick with appropriate glazing. It is all rather Germanic! (See illus 39.) Now converted into a very special sort of holiday cottage, it sleeps three. There is one room on each of the four floors: bathroom, kitchen, living room and bedroom as one ascends. The top of the roof is surmounted by a weathervane in the form of a squirrel, which is the crest of the Gilbert family, the tower having been built by Carew Davies Gilbert. Sir Humphrey Gilbert of Compton Castle (qv), the discoverer of Newfoundland, named his ship *Squirrel*.

28 Trelissick New Lodge

This is a charming essay in Victorian picturesque architecture, typical of what the best houses chose to adorn their main gate! It was built about 1870 by the Gilbert family and sleeps four.

Trevarrian, near Mawgan Porth

29 Beacon House

Trevarrian is a hamlet on the B3276 coast road that links Newquay and Padstow, and is three-quarters of a mile south of Mawgan Porth. Beacon House has been divided into two, West House to sleep four, and East House to sleep five.

Veryan

30 Parc Behan Cottage

Park Behan in the attractive village of Veryan was built about a century and a half ago by the then incumbent of the parish. This cottage, where the groom lived, sleeps four.

31 Gwendra Farm House

This south Cornish farmhouse is immediately above Pendower Beach (see page 50) and has been divided into two flats: the upper one sleeps six, the lower one five.

Launceston Museum

Lawrence House, 9 Castle Street (built in 1753), was given to the Trust in 1964 by Mrs G. W. Kittow with the intention that it should be preserved, thus helping to conserve the character of a street which has a number of good Georgian brick houses, notably Castle Hill House and nos 3–13.

The house is now let to Launceston Town Council and is used as the Mayor's Parlour and Museum, containing much of local life through the centuries. There are reproductions of coins struck at Launceston Mint in the reign of Aethelred (978–1016), and from prehistoric times, stones, pottery and bones from a local Bronze Age burial discovered in 1973, a Bronze Age axe head, and an Iron Age pot in perfect condition. The armoury contains a fine seventeenth century wheel-lock sporting rifle, and there are paintings and drawings of Launceston Castle. Among the uniforms is a rare one of the Launceston and Newport Volunteers dating from Napoleonic times. The Victorian period is represented by dresses, kitchen tools and implements, including an 1844 local john-box clock. The feudal dues presented to the Duke of Cornwall on his visit in 1973 are also on display.

Wayside Cottages, St Agnes

These three cottages, typical of mid-Cornwall, were given to the Trust in 1944 during World War II. They are stone built with slate roofs. They are not open to the public, but can be seen at the northeast end of Beaconsfield Place 70yd west of the parish church.

Old Post Office, Tintagel

The Introduction has recorded the arrival of the Trust in Cornwall at Tintagel in the 1890s, when this historic place was in the full flush of the popularity brought about by the poetry of Alfred, Lord Tennyson, Matthew Arnold and Algernon Swinburne, all of whom had contributed to its 'aura' in the minds of Victorian Romantics. Arthur Salmon wrote in 1903

> 'It has a distinct claim to be the most famous spot in the duchy. It had a wide reputation long before the railway, and Welsh bards, Breton minstrels and British chroniclers had all assisted to spread abroad the tale of Arthur and Tintagel.'

The disastrous result of this popularity can be seen in the village and its environs today. The old cottages were ruthlessly torn down and replaced by boarding houses, shops and hotels: eg, 'King Arthur Arms landlord John Wade Smith' in 1873. Even Arthur Mee was to write in *Cornwall, The King's England* in 1937 'Tintagel has thrown away its glory and deserves no reputation. It is a long unlovely street'. But see illus 40, one of Francis Frith's photographs probably taken in the 1890s and showing the post office. 150 years ago, letters for Tintagel were brought by foot-

messenger from the turnpike road at Camelford 6 miles away where they had arrived by coach. After Rowland Hill's introduction of the penny post in 1840, there was an improvement of postal arrangements in the remotest of country places, and in 1844 the GPO decided to establish a Letter Receiving Office for the district and chose Trevena, nowadays called Tintagel, as the most central place in a scattered parish of 7 square miles. A room was rented from the owner of the old Trevena Manor House and the office was set up. In 1892, the owner decided to sell the building for redevelopment and gave the GPO notice to quit. For almost half a century the place had served as the village post office, and it has since been known as the Old Post Office.

Three years later, it was put up for auction, and a group of artists were so concerned that one of them, Catherine Johns, purchased it on the understanding that means would be found to preserve it. Sales of pictures took place to provide money for repairs, and in 1900 the Trust agreed to buy it from Miss Johns for £100 which was raised by a public appeal. It was subject to a lease to her for life, and finally vested in the Trust in 1903, the Trust's second acquisition in Cornwall.

The Old Post Office has a plan approximating to that of a manor house c 1450, and it is an interesting and rare survival of an early

Illus 40 A Frith photograph of the 1890s of Tintagel showing the Trevena Manor House on the left. It was used as the post office 1844–92

domestic dwelling in Cornwall. It is built of local slate, and its heavy 'rag' slates have bent the rafters to give a wildly uneven roof. The chimney stacks are provided with slate drips capped with a 'pot' consisting of four slates set on edge.

The entrance passage, which runs right through to the garden, is like the screens passage in a grander building. On the right is the parlour from where a narrow steep stair leads up to the parlour chamber, ie bedroom. The ground floor hall rises to the full height of the house, out of which is the post room, recently refurnished as a Victorian village post office (see illus 41). The telegraph wires arrived in Tintagel in 1890, and on the counter is a Spagnoletti receiver and undulator of the period.

The initial restoration was carried out in 1903 for the Trust by the well-known architect Detmar Blow, and it was again restored and officially opened on 2 June 1971. In 1976 24,000 visitors came to see it.

Illus 41   Tintagel: old post office

10 Industrial Archaeology

DEVON

Arlington Court

A splendid assortment of horsedrawn vehicles are housed in the stables.

Buckland Abbey

In addition to the horse-drawn vehicles housed in the tithe barn (see page 66) there is also to be seen a farm cider-press about 290 years old, and a hand litter or hand-drawn ambulance of 1913.

The main building houses a Folk Museum, containing a collection of tools and other artifacts of rural crafts, and the Naval Gallery with a considerable collection of prints, ship models and other marine items.

Beesands Cliff, Torcross

The details of the old slate quarry are to be found on page 30.

Branscombe

Near the social hall, about 350yd northeast of the parish church, is the disused village smithy. On the opposite side of the road, up the side of a stream and across a bridge, is the village bakery, where the ovens are still fired by faggots, and produce *real* crusty bread. Both H. J. Massingham and W. H. Hudson have written lovingly of the life of this rural community, where the great Walter Bronescombe, Bishop of Exeter, was born in the thirteenth century.

Lundy Island

For details of the three lighthouses and church see page 23.

Plym Bridge Woods

Traversing the length of these woods is a mile of the track of the former GWR Plymouth–Tavistock–Launceston branch railway line, originally laid in 1858–9. The Cann Viaduct is not Trust property.

From a point a quarter of a mile northwest of the gate at the Plym Bridge entrance to these woods, and running northwards, the track can be followed for over three-quarters of a mile of the old Plymouth and Dartmoor Railway originally opened in 1823 and taken up in 1916, although it had been disused long before that date. It skirts the top (western) edge of Rumple Quarry, west of the Cann Viaduct. For other details, see page 118.

Wheal Betsy

Four miles northeast of Tavistock on the A386, the main road to Okehampton, and lying below and to the east of the road, is the splendid beam engine house of Wheal Betsy. There is a tremendous back-cloth of Dartmoor to the east, and Gibbet Hill rises to 1158ft on the west. It is marked 'Chy' on the 1in Ordnance Survey map.

Northeast of the building a stream rises at Chalwell, and after the mine was re-opened in 1806, there was sufficient head of water to turn two 50ft waterwheels. The ore raised was lead containing silver. In 1868, the engine house was built to house a large beam engine, which continued in use until the works closed in 1877. In earlier years, the miners raised 400 tons of ore a year, yielding 4000–5000 ounces of silver.

At a later date, the engine house came into the possession of the South Western Electricity Board via a local company after nationalisation, and the Board was asked by the Army for permission to blow it up as a miliary exercise. There was, rightly, a public outcry, and the building was given to the Cornish Engines Preservation Society, who in turn gave it to the Trust in 1967. A grant from the Historic Buildings Council enabled the Trust to restore the engine house, using its own staff, at a cost of about £1000 in 1968.

CORNWALL

Boscastle Harbour

The curving jetty was built by Sir Richard Grenville in 1584, but the harbour is a lot older since the Duchy of Cornwall Havener (Harbour Master) let it at £1 per annum from 1337 onwards as a port in the Hundred of Trigg. A pier had been erected in 1547 but it was soon in a bad condition, and Grenville rebuilt it 'in a newe place'. This is the curving jetty of today. It was again rebuilt by Cotton Amy in 1740, and in the nineteenth century corn, slate from Delabole, manganese ore from mines near Altarnun and, after 1865, china clay were exported. Imports were hardware, pottery, coal, manure and limestone.

The outer breakwater was built c 1820, but blown up by a drifting mine in 1941, and one of the Trust's tasks on acquiring the harbour in 1962 was to rebuild it. No contractor could be found willing to do the job and the work was done by the Trust's own masons, backed up by a team of gardeners and woodmen from Cotehele who worked in icy weather between tides, often soaked to the skin, for an entire winter. They completed the job to the consternation of local wiseacres who said 't'wasn't possible'. The Trust also owns the Palace Stables at the harbour head, where the carthorses which operated the capstans were stabled. This unique Cornish harbour is still used by fishermen bound for the valuable shell-fish ground south of Hartland Point. The Old Forge and the limekiln, both in Trust ownership, can also be seen.

Carleon Cove, Ruan Minor

For the details of the Lizard Serpentine Company's factory in this tiny cove, see page 47, Chapter 4. Still to be seen is the wheel pit, the ruins of one building, a roofed warehouse with an 1866 datestone, and a large block of stone, covered with long grooves and set into the ground. This was where the huge blocks of serpentine were sawn into slabs by water power, to be used for facing buildings and for such internal uses as fireplace surrounds.

Cornish Engines

If someone had predicted to the founders of the National Trust in 1895 that a steam engine (then a mere three years old pumping water out of a Cornish tin mine) would become part of their heritage sixty years later, they would have been astonished. But this has happened, and not only one engine but five are now cared for by the Trust; great steam machines that were an integral part of Cornish mining for 250 years.

The Cornish beam engine evolved from a very simple machine, the once common backyard hand-pump over the head of a well. The hand is applied to a rod connected with a pivoted lever; as the rod is lifted and lowered so the plunger, fixed to the other end of the lever is raised and lowered in the well, discharging water from the pump faucet.

In the beam engine, the rod is an immense piston in a cylinder driven by steam pressure. The pivoted lever is a huge rocking beam, half inside and half outside the engine house, and the plunger in a pumping engine is a very long rod that goes down the mine shaft. As it is raised and lowered, so the waste water in the mine is discharged. The engine works in a vertical plane, and so there evolved the tall building or engine house that has become part of the Cornish mining landscape.

The earliest engines, invented by a Dartmouth toolmaker, Thomas Newcomen, were made in Queen Anne's reign. Visitors to the Trust's coast site at Little Dartmouth will find it rewarding to go and see an actual Newcomen engine in working order in an engine house near the quay. A plaque in the building states that it was built about 1725, with iron parts made at the cradle of the Industrial Revolution, the Darby Foundry at Coalbrookdale, Shropshire. It worked until 1913, and was moved in 1963 from Hawkesbury Canal Junction near Coventry to Dartmouth to commemorate the tercentenary of Newcomen's birth.

At the peak period of the mining industry in Cornwall, 1850–60, there were about 650 beam engines working plus another 60 in the western part of Devon, and even more in Somerset. They represented a colossal output from the Cornish foundries and were developed from the inventive genius of Cornish engineer Richard Trevithick (1771–1833). In the 1790s he visited the Darby Foundry several times and the iron craftsmen there built to his design the first locomotives in the world in the years 1802–4. He was the pioneer of high-pressure steam, using pressures up to 100lb per square inch, unheard of until then. He is reported to have said 'My predecessors put their boiler into the fire, I have put my fire into the boiler'. So successful was the development of the Cornish engine that the annual tonnage of tin produced rose from 2500 tons in 1750 to 14000 in 1860, quite apart from the far greater amounts of copper being mined at the same time, plus lead and other metals.

By the 1920s, there were only about twenty engines left at work in Cornwall, and in 1935 the discovery that a very historic engine near Pendeen in the far southwest was about to be sold for scrap prompted the formation of a Committee who saved it for posterity.

Out of this action, the Cornish Engines Preservation Society was formed, and in turn five engines were saved. In 1964 the Trust offered to accept the task of preservation if money to repair the buildings and endow them for the future could be found. Two years later, the Historic Buildings Council made a grant of £3000 for immediate assistance in repairing and refurbishing four engines, an engine house in West Devon at Wheal Betsy (see page 152), and Trevithick's cottage at Penponds near Camborne. Further money was then raised, and the Society conveyed its property to the Trust in 1967.

The engines and other buildings now cared for by the Trust are located in various places.

1 East Pool Winding Engine

This is the most conspicuous engine to be seen today, on the south side of the A3074 at Pool between Redruth and Camborne. It was built at Holman's Foundry, Camborne, in 1887, and was the last rotative beam winding engine made in Cornwall. It operated at East Pool Mine from 1887 to 1920 when the mine closed, and remained in its engine house becoming gradually more derelict. Since the Trust has cared for it, it has been put into first class condition, and on 20 August 1975, the Lady Anne Boles, wife of the Director General of the Trust, performed the opening ceremony of the re-working of the engine by electric power. It has a 30in diameter cylinder and a stroke of 9ft.

2 East Pool Pumping Engine

This is the largest and youngest of all the engines left in Cornwall, and lies a quarter of a mile northeast of the winding engine. This great machine, its cylinder 90in in diameter, weighs 125 tons. The designer was Nicholas Trestrail, whose son-in-law Mr Maynard was present at the opening of the winding engine in 1975. It was built by Harvey & Co of Hayle, and set to work in 1892 at Carn Brea Mine. In 1923 it was purchased by the East Pool and Agar Mining Company, re-erected in a brand-new engine house the following year and re-started in 1925. It finally stopped thirty years later.

This engine represents the peak of development of the Cornish beam engines (see illus 42). Its stroke is 10ft, and the huge beam or 'bob' to use the Cornish name weighs 52 tons. The pumping rod descends into the shaft for a distance of 1700ft, and the total weight of water in motion in the shaft at every engine stroke was 85 tons, and with a stroke every 12 seconds, about 27000 gallons an hour were discharged. Both these engines are open to visitors.

Illus 42   The beam pumping engine at East Pool made in 1892 and re-erected here in 1924. Attached to the pumping rod is the beam of the balance box taken from another engine of 1911

3 Robinson's Engine : South Crofty Mine

This active mine, three-quarters of a mile southwest of the two East Pool engines, has another and much older engine at Robinson's Shaft. It was commissioned in 1853 from the Copperhouse Foundry at Hayle, and designed by Samuel Grose, a pupil of Trevithick. Its cylinder is 80in in diameter.

It first worked at Great Wheal Alfred near Hayle 1854–64, then moved to Wheal Abraham 5 miles away, working there until 1875. It was again moved in 1882 by a huge team of horses to Tregurtha Downs Mine near Marazion, where it worked until 1898. Four years later, it was moved to South Crofty and restarted in 1903, pumping 340 gallons a minute from 2021ft until it was over a hundred years old. It finally stopped on 1 May 1955, and is a veritable giant of the steam age. It can only be inspected by written application to South Crofty Limited as it is at the head of a working shaft.

4 Rostowrack Engine

This is a very unusual engine, in that whilst it is a rotative engine like East Pool usually used for winding, it was used to pump liquid china-clay slurry from the sump of a clay-pit up to the surface. The pump rod was activated by the use of a bell-crank and flat rods which translated the circular motion of the flywheel into horizontal motion.

It has a 22in cylinder, and was made at West and Sons Foundry at St Blazey in 1851. First set to work at a clay works at Locking Gate near Bugle, it was moved in 1861 to the Rostowrack clay pit where it did duty continuously for ninety-one years until retired in 1952. It was owned by the Goonvean and Rostowrack China Clay Co Ltd whose Chairman was Lord Falmouth, and through the kindness of Holman Bros it was re-erected in their museum at Camborne in 1953, where it operates by compressed air.

5 Levant Engine

The famous Levant mine, right on the cliff edge north of St Just, operated from 1820 to 1930, and when this engine was saved from the blowtorch in 1935, it was realised that here was a very historic winding engine, made at the Harvey Foundry in Hayle in 1840. Its cylinder is 24in in diameter and the stroke 4ft.

It is housed in an old stone engine house on the extreme edge of the cliff 1 mile west of Pendeen, and is in an extremely vulnerable position. It is very costly to maintain, work constantly being needed both inside and out. It can only be inspected by written application to the manager of Geevor Mine nearby.

Trevithick's Cottage

Just under a mile southwest of Camborne is the village of Penponds, and here is the cottage where Richard Trevithick lived between 1810 and 1815 and where his father died in 1797 and his mother in 1810. Since the Trust took it over, the roof has been re-thatched, and new floors have been provided throughout. It has a commemorative tin plaque on the west gable an 1 can be visited upon request to the private tenant.

Wheal Coates Engine House, St Agnes

On the cliff edge, west of St Agnes Beacon and north of Chapel Porth, lies the deserted and very ancient tin mine of Wheal Coates. 200ft above the sea is the pumping engine house of the Towanwroath Shaft built c 1860 and higher up the cliff lies the impressive ruin of the winding and stamps engine houses. To stand on the cliff top and look down at the pumping engine house is to experience a little of the indomitable spirit of the Cornish miner. This mine finally stopped on 17 March 1914. (See illus 43.)

A little over half a mile south-south-east of Towanwroath Shaft is a smaller engine house on the southwest slope of Chapel Coombe. This was the pumping engine of the long disused Charlotte United Mine, worked for tin and copper in the 1830s. On the Trust's land here there is a huge tract of old mining waste, interspersed with shafts, running from Towan Cross to the coast at Mulgran Hill, the 'deads' of Wheal Charlotte and Charlotte United, sometimes also known as North Towan Mine.

Wheal Prosper, Breage

This was part of the Marazion Mines group, and yielded £60,000 of copper ore between 1832–49. The engine house (c 1830) lies above a 600ft deep shaft, and when the Trust acquired it in 1969, it had been showing signs of collapse for a decade. It was decided to restore it, an appeal was launched and R. F. Pascoe and Son of Breage carried out the work for £4,000; started in 1970 it has now been completed. The Trust has made a car park a quarter of a mile northwest.

Cotehele Mill and Quay

This historic estate was quite self-contained for centuries, and its corn mill would have been a vital part of its economy. It is called Morden Mill on the older 6in Ordnance Survey map and is powered by the Morden stream that rises at Silverhill 4 miles to the west. On its way to the Tamar, the stream powered four mills, Morden being the last. Provender milling went on here until 1965. It has been the manor mill since early medieval times, and the present building probably dates from the eighteenth century.

Illus 43 Part of the pumping engine house at Wheal Coates, St Agnes

The holiday cottage which is part of the building was at one time the workshop where fruit punnets were made, a second waterwheel providing the power for the saw. The steep sloping sides of the Tamar Valley have been used for growing cherries and strawberries for about 140 years and so fertile were they that 100 acres produced 400 tons of strawberries per year. It was indeed aptly called the Vale of Plenty. The punnets were made at 144 (one gross) for a shilling (5p), and Cotehele Quay was the collection centre for fruit, which was ferried across to the Devon bank at 1d ($\frac{1}{2}$p) per box and thence by horsedrawn cart to Bere Alston Station when the railway was opened in 1890.

Also at the mill, which has been put into complete working order, see the wheelwright's shop, with all its special tools, the forge, and the cider mill inside part of the mill.

Cotehele Quay is a splendid example of a large quay on a tidal river with its limekiln and crane. This particular example made in 1865 came from Hennett Spink and Else's foundry at Bridge-water, and is of a type used by the Cornwall Railway and seen until recently in many country station yards. On the quay is a branch of the National Maritime Museum, and the Trust's first ship is in the dock. This is the Tamar ketch-rigged barge, *Shamrock*, (see illus 44) which is being rebuilt. It was made in 1899, and sailed up and down the river for nearly seventy years.

Angrouse Cliff, Mullion

See Chapter 4, p 46 for details of Marconi's Wireless Station site.

Mullion Harbour

For details see Chapter 4, p 46.

Penberth Cove

The Trust owns here a working capstan for hauling small fishing boats up the beach, a rare survival.

Pentireglaze

On this headland overlooking Pentireglaze Haven, the farm of the same name was acquired in 1973. On it are the 'burrows' of the ancient Pentire Glaze Mine which produced antimony and lead, and was famous for its specimens of cerussite (lead carbonate). It was recorded as far back as 1580 and was last worked about 1857.

St Michael's Mount

For details of the harbour and underground railway see Chapter 6, pp 96 and 99.

Trelissick Water Tower

For details see Chapter 9, p 146.

Pont Quay

A chart of the 'Fowey Roads' dated 1786 shows, opposite Fowey town, Polheath Point and the entrance to Pont Pill. A mile up-stream, navigable at high water, is Pont Quay now owned by the Trust. This was an old schooner quay, as a notice dated May 1894 bears witness: 'Dues for shipping over these quays Grain 1d per quarter, Manure 3d per ton, Sand 2d, Coal 3d'. It is signed by William Pease of Lostwithiel who was 'Commissioner in all the common law courts and secretary to the River Fowey Conservancy Board'.

The Trust also has a fascinating saw mill powered by a water-wheel and, typical of a creek head, a kiln for burning limestone brought in schooners from Oreston, Plymouth.

Illus 44   The Tamar barge *Shamrock* built in 1899 and now under reconstruction at Cotehele Quay

11 Prehistoric Sites

DEVON

Hembury Woods, Buckfastleigh

On the 500ft summit is Hembury Castle which is an Iron Age hill fort, and inside the wall the mutilated motte and bailey of the later Dane's Castle. The site covers 7 acres and the fort has three ramparts, (see p 109).

Ilfracombe

On Damage Cliffs, southeast of Bull Point, are two standing stones (menhirs) of the Bronze Age c 1500 BC.

Lundy

Antiquities of the Mesolithic, Bronze and Iron Ages which have been discovered on the island include flints, hut sites and a kistvaen; Dark Age pottery of imported Mediterranean hard red ware has been found and, most important, four Early Christian memorial stones, establishing Lundy high on the list of Early Christian sites in Britain. The first was found in 1905 and in 1923 its inscription was read as '*Igerni . . . I. Tigerni*'. The other three stones have been found since 1962, the inscriptions being *Potiti*, *Optimi*, and *Resenat*. All four date from the fifth–sixth centuries AD.

Lynmouth

Between Lynmouth and Countisbury and crossing the main A39 coast road at Wind Hill is an early Iron Age linear earthwork 450yd in length running northwest from the top of Chisel Coombe to the cliff edge above Sillery Sands on the west side of Foreland Point. On the spur of Myrtlebury are two defensive earthworks, not necessarily associated or contemporary.

Mortehoe

The land at Baggy Point at the southern end of Morte Bay has yielded flints, some of them dating from the Mesolithic period ie c 6000–5000 BC, but also some dating from the Neolithic and Bronze Ages 4000–1000 BC.

Salcombe

On the summit of Bolt Tail above Hope Cove there are traces of an Iron Age promontory fort c 500 BC.

Yelverton

On the Goodameavy property, there are the remains of an Iron Age promontory fort on the Dewerstone Rock; Early and Middle Bronze Age hut circles on Wigford Down adjoining the Trust's northeast boundary; and, to be seen in Plymouth City Museum, an unusual pottery cup which was found at Dewerstone in 1960.

Hentor and Trowlesworthy

This large moorland area is positively 'littered' with antiquities, all dating from the Bronze Age c 2000–1000 BC (see page 110). The visitor is recommended to explore armed with the larger scale 6in Ordnance Survey maps.

CORNWALL

Boscastle

See page 36 for the 'stitch-meal' plots on Forrabury Common.

Callington

See page 121 for the early Iron Age hill fort (probable) at Cadson Bury in St Ive parish.

Camelford

The Rough Tor settlement site is a well-preserved group of hut-circles and associated structures, including (conjectured) cornplots outlined by stone baulks and with indications of lynchets, downland grass terraces formed as a result of prehistoric ploughings.

Gorran

On the 373ft summit of Dodman Point is an Iron Age promontory fort, and a very deep defensive ditch called the Bulwark or Balk.

Cubert

On Kelsey Head, there is a promontory fort or cliff castle.

Gunwalloe

On Mullion golf course, the site of which is owned by the Trust, there are several barrows or tumuli, but watch out for rapidly moving golf balls!

Pentire Point, Padstow

The Rumps on Rumps Point is a cliff castle enclosing about 6 acres, and bounded on the south by three ramparts and ditches.

Excavations since 1963 have yielded pottery fragments including cordoned urns of northwest France type, and of a western Mediterranean type of amphora, predominantly first century BC.

Lanyon Quoit, Penzance

This is a monument of the Neolithic Age which is dated between 1500–1000 BC and is a chamber tomb. There are four in southwest Cornwall of which Lanyon is one; locally called cromlechs or quoits, they are vestiges of burial chambers, made of massive upright stone slabs with a flat roofing slab. They were originally concealed within large barrows of earth or stone, the outlines of which can sometimes be traced.

Lanyon is a Penwith (the name of the district) chamber tomb, probably an Irish-inspired derivative of the 'gallery grave' type of tomb, and was once covered by a long mound 80–90ft in length and 40ft wide. It ran north and south, with the chamber at the northern end.

The group of four great stones, best described as a huge three-legged table, are the result of a re-erection in 1824 following a collapse in 1815, and the original was higher than the present group.

Keen photographers may like to photograph this most-visited of all the Penwith cromlechs by siting the camera so that through two of the upright slabs is seen, half a mile due north, another great monument, the building that housed the beam pumping engine at the head of the Greenburrow Shaft of the Ding Dong mine, last used in 1878.

St Agnes

On the Beacon there are a number of tumuli.

Park Head, St Eval

Half a mile northeast of the headland is a group of six tumuli (barrows) of the round type.

St Keverne

1¼ miles across the bay northeast of Coverack is Lowland Point, where the Trust owns 57 acres of farmland and wild cliffs. Here is a raised beach which is a relic of the Ice Age. The cliffs of the former coast rise to 250ft in the escarpment half a mile inland.

St Michael's Mount

In the absence of excavation, it is not yet possible to say what prehistoric remains there may be on this island. There appears to be some evidence that it was the place called Ictis, and on the mainland the remains of a smelting pit have been found, together with portions of a bronze cauldron surrounded by ashes, charcoal and slag, and the refuse of smelted ores. Ictis was the port from which Cornish tin was exported to Greek trading communities in the Mediterranean.

There is however one artifact on the Mount about which questions are always asked, the small stone lion carved out of a species of red granite that guards the north terrace by the church. It was brought from Sinai by Sir John St Aubyn in the nineteenth century. It came originally from Karnak in Upper Egypt, the site of the City of Thebes, and was dated by the British Museum to c 400 BC.

Sennen

Chapel Carn Brea, see Chapter 8, p 121. Maen Castle, see Chapter 3, p 41.

Tintagel

There is a cliff castle on the southwest flank of Willapark above Gullastem.

Trelissick

Half a mile north of the mansion, two creeks meet the Fal river: Coombe coming in from the northwest, and Lamouth from the west. At the point formed by their junction is Roundwood promontory fort, a particularly interesting example which guarded the approach to these creeks from the south. There is an old lane from Tregew used at one time by horsedrawn vehicles going to and from the old Roundwood Fort Quay, one of several riverside quays which existed when there was schooner and barge traffic on the river between Falmouth and Truro.

Trencrom

See Chapter 8, p 129.

Treryn-dinas

See Chapter 4, page 43.

Veryan

On the Trust's Pendower property is Carne Beacon, three quarters of a mile south-south-west of Veryan church. Charles Henderson, perhaps Cornwall's greatest twentieth century historian, says of it 'by far the largest bowl barrow in Cornwall is the great tumulus at Carn in Veryan. It must be one of the biggest in Great Britain.'

It is 372ft in circumference and 570ft above sea level, and is traditionally the burial place of King Gerennius or Gereint (Welsh: Geraint) of Cornwall c AD 589. An excavation in 1855 revealed a kistvaen with the ashes of 'the old king enclosed in a rude stone chest' (*The Handbook for Travellers*). Some authorities link Carne Beacon with an earthwork called 'Dingerein Castel' 2 miles to the southwest. A quarter of a mile northwest of the Beacon is another earthwork known as the Castle.

Nature Reserves

1 Arlington Court, North Devon

In the park are Shetland ponies, donkeys and a flock of Jacob sheep, following the practice established by Miss Rosalie Chichester who made the park and indeed much of her estate into an animal sanctuary and nature reserve, protecting plants and animals including deer. That practice is still being followed by the Trust and Arlington lake to the southeast of the park is a wildfowl sanctuary.

2 Clovelly, North Devon

Nearly a quarter of the Trust's property at The Brownshams, 2 miles northwest of Clovelly, is managed as a nature reserve.

3 Ardevora, South Cornwall

The Trust's 54 acres here, for topography see Chapter 8 p 120, are leased to the Cornwall Naturalists' Trust for Nature Conservation. The area comprises saltmarsh and muddy fore-shore. There is typical saltmarsh vegetation and a feeding ground for birds.

4 Kynance Cliffs and Lower Predannack Downs, Lizard

215 acres here are leased to the Cornwall Naturalists' Trust; mainly heathland on serpentine rock with the unique Lizard flora.

5 Lower Predannack Cliff and Mullion Island, Lizard

41 acres here are leased to the Cornwall Naturalists' Trust; mainly heathy cliff slopes on horn-blende schists with typical vegetation. There are breeding seabirds on the island.

6 Peter's Wood, Boscastle, North Cornwall

25 acres here are leased to the Cornwall Naturalists' Trust; north-facing deciduous wood with sessile oaks, ground flora and a stream.

Epilogue

The National Trust is a charity. The preservation of all that it owns and safeguards for the nation – countryside, coast and buildings— is ultimately dependent on the support of its members. This book has endeavoured to describe just how much of the heritage of Devon and Cornwall is in fact cared for by the Trust, 40,000 acres of land, more than 150 miles of fine coastline, and twelve great houses to say the least.

Without the Trust, much that remains of our heritage would have decayed or been destroyed. Still more must be safeguarded. This independent society, acting for the nation, is able to ensure that its buildings and land are safe for all time. It is now costing about £10 million a year to run, much of the money being provided by endowments whilst visitors' fees bring in over £1 million. The members' subscriptions are vital, and *many more are needed*. Membership helps all those who love Britain to become personally involved in conservation. In 1973, the historic buildings belonging to the Trust attracted five million visitors, and in 1976, the total number of overseas tourists to Britain reached ten million, about 10 per cent more than in 1975 when Britain earned a total of £1439 million in foreign currency from nine million tourists.

In 1945, when the Trust reached its half-century, G. M. Trevelyan OM wrote:

'Destruction walks by the noon-day. Unless there is a reversal of the era of destruction, and the conservation of beauty taken in hand, then the future of our race, whatever its social, economic and political structure may be, will be shorn of spiritual value. To this great work of salvage, the National Trust makes, at least, a contribution'.

That was written more than thirty years ago when the Trust's *total* estate was 110,000 acres, with 40,000 more protected by covenants, ie properties not owned by the Trust but whose amenities are protected by restrictive covenants which the owners have given to the Trust or which the Trust have purchased. Such land or buildings cannot, however, benefit from the protection against compulsory acquisition that is enjoyed by land held by the Trust as *inalienable*. This unique power was conferred by parliament upon the Trust as far back as 1907 and the majority of its properties are inalienable; they can *never* be sold or mortgaged, nor compulsorily acquired without the special will of parliament. The Devon and Cornwall estate is now 40,000 acres, and about 8,000 more are covenanted.

May Sir John Summerson have the last word

'So much depends on the loyalty of old families to their traditional homes, on the initiative of institutions (like the National Trust) in turning old fabrics to new uses, on the sense of responsibility of local authorities, and in the last resort on the ordinary citizen whose concern with history and sense of wonder are the justification of the whole matter.'

This Guide, it is hoped, is a better interpretation of all that the Trust cares for in Devon and Cornwall, not only on behalf of its peoples, but for all those who visit the area. It surely underwrites the international award of the Johann Wolfgang von Goethe Gold Medal given to the Trust in November 1977 by the FVS Foundation, Hamburg, for the splendid example it has set for the whole of Europe in the conservation of architectural heritage and landscape.

Acknowledgements

The author is extremely grateful to many officers and others connected with The National Trust for their help and encouragement in writing this book, and in particular to Michael Trinick and Warren Davis of Saltram, and to Richard Meyrick and Julian Prideaux, the Agents for Devon and Cornwall.

He also expresses his thanks to the many persons who gave of their time either in interviews or by correspondence that was of so much help in the preparation of this Guide.

The Illustrations

Illus no 32 is reproduced here by kind permission of *Country Life*. The National Trust kindly lent all of the photographs including those taken by: G. F. Allen (no 3); John Bethell (no 18); Ray Bishop (nos 11, 41, 42); Robert Chapman (nos 20, 28, 44); Herbert Felton (no 25); F. Frith & Co (nos 1, 40); Nicholas Horne Ltd (no 9); A. F. Kersting (no 12); Morgan Whale and Mallett (no 30); John Owen (no 6); Photo Precision Ltd (no 22); J. Pounder (no 35); Severn-Smith Photographic (no 34); Nicholas Toyne of Jerome Dessain & Co (nos 2, 4, 5, 8, 13, 17, 18); Charles Woolf (nos 10, 33, 39, 43). The floor plans are reproduced from the National Trust's booklets and the map was drawn by Vic Welch.

Index

Page numbers in italic type refer to illustrations. The abbreviation HC after a page number indicates a reference to one of the Trust's holiday cottages.